WITHOUT LUCK

a book about innovation

david hoyt
d13 publishing

David Hoyt is the founder of d13 innovation consulting,
a strategy firm that supports people who bring the best innovations into the world.

d13, San Diego 92198
© 2017 by David Hoyt
withoutluck.com

All rights reserved.
Published October 21, 2017.
Printed in the United States of America

Edited by John Cannon
Cover Design by JeromeLacote.com

ISBN-10: 1979099936
ISBN-13: 978-1979099936

Without Luck

Contents

INTRODUCTION 1
OVERVIEW 3
Part 1: DEFINING INNOVATION 5
Reasoning by Analogy 7
Reasoning by First Principles 11
Secrets About People 13
Secrets About Nature 17
Infinite Innovation 21
Intro to The Gang 27
Part 2: INNOVATION GRADES 35
Innovation Rating System 39
Grades AAA, AA, A 43
Grade B—Mimetic 51
Grade C—The Wave 57
Grade D—Decade 65
Industry Application of the Six Grades 71
Introduction to Bond Ratings 77
Part 3: INNOVATION TYPES 81
Products 83
Funding 97
Information 105
Brand 109
Channel 119
Network 127
Core Process 135
Enabling Process 143
Economies of Scale 149
Culture 153
Governance 163
Customer Engagement and Service 167

Complex Coordination 173

Part 4: PEOPLE **177**
Expertise and Motivation 179
Creatives 183
Supporting Roles 187
Mismatched Roles 191

Part 5: ORGANIZATIONAL STRUCTURES **199**

Part 6: DIFFUSION PROCESS **209**
Adopters 211
Non-Adopters 217
Social Systems 221
Diffusion Process 229

EPILOGUE **241**

Appendix **243**
Markus 245
Sarah 261
Joko 277
Questionnaire 293

About the Author **301**

Notes **303**

INTRODUCTION

Who makes a bet if they don't know how it's gonna turn out?
— Bobby Axelrod, *Billions*

Have you ever known someone who is lucky? Getting lucky is a seductive story. Luck makes you feel like any day it will come around the corner, wink at you and take you for the ride of your life. Luck also protects you, as it whispers in your ear that the only thing standing in your way is the one thing you can't control.

Innovation initiatives and startups are full of stories about luck, but these stories do more harm than good because they trick you. These stories make you feel like your lucky break is inevitable. They make you feel like your hard work and dedication have earned you the luck you need to achieve your vision. They teach that innovation is a random series of events, and if you keep buying raffle tickets, you will eventually win. Luck is a lie and doesn't exist.

The reality is innovation works in a very predictable way. Good strategy looks like good luck to the outsider, and bad strategy looks like bad luck to the insider. I have unlocked the secrets of innovation, so that you can plan and execute with confidence. Risks exist, of course, but I can show you where they are so you will know what to expect.

Without Luck gives you the tools to craft good innovation strategy. By the time you finish the book, you will be prepared to create a concise, one-page innovation strategy, from beginning to end. Without luck.

OVERVIEW

The truth is rarely pure and never simple.
— Oscar Wilde, *The Importance of Being Earnest*

This book is organized in six parts. Each part builds on the others to give you a complete understanding that enables you to create the best strategy for your idea.

Part 1: Defining Innovation

You learn: How to generate good ideas and how the definition of innovation and its effects influence your approach. I use the laws of economics and physics to explain how scarcity, supply and demand, pricing, order, disorder, scarcity, and systems define innovation.

Part 2: Innovation Grades

You learn: How to tell which ideas will fail, even before they launch. The Innovation Rating System is six grades defined by benefits and risks. Finally you have a common language to assess mutually exclusive speculative projects against sure shots.

Part 3: Innovation Types

You learn: Where and how to improve your own idea. Whenever people organize they must solve three categories of problems: characteristics of the product or service they provide, internal operations, and distribution of the product or service. These categories spawn thirteen types of innovations.

Part 4: People

You learn: Who you need on your team to succeed and who you are missing when things go wrong. There are four kinds of people to consider when forming the right team. Get these wrong and failure is inevitable.

Part 5: Organizational Structures

You learn: How you improve your odds of success. Speed is essential to the execution of innovation and the organizational structure you choose dictates how fast you can move.

Part 6: Diffusion Process

You learn: How you communicate with customers is different in each of the four phases of product/market fit. I give you the tools to dissect the social dynamics of your customers so you can help them adopt your innovation.

PART 1: DEFINING INNOVATION

You can't treat all good ideas the same way. The most important concept to know about innovation is that your approach matters just as much as the idea. Your execution is a combination of strategy and tactics. Strategy is an overall plan and tactics are the things you do to make the strategy work. Tactics are popular because they are easily understood. Tactics are visible to outsiders and insiders because they are actions that require coordination, communication, materials, and people both inside and outside the organization. Strategy is less visible to outsiders and insiders because it is the arrangement and combination of all these open actions to achieve an objective. Strategy is often planned in secret and rolled out over a long period of time.

I want you to create a strong strategy based on the uniqueness of your idea so that your tactics are consistent and work toward your objectives.

The two useful ways of thinking about innovation and creating a good strategy are to learn from what others have done, and to examine fundamental truths so you can create something from scratch. Both approaches extend across the innovation process whether you are evaluating ideas, creating a strategy to improve execution, identifying solutions when problems arise, or even explaining failed initiatives.

Elon Musk, the founder of Tesla Inc., contrasted these two particular ways of thinking in his TED interview in March 2013, conducted by Chris Anderson.

> *I do think there is a good framework for thinking. It is physics — you know the sort of first principles reasoning. What I mean by that is it boils things down to their fundamental truths and reason up from there as opposed to reasoning by analogy. Through most of our life, we get through it by reasoning through analogy, which essentially means copying what other people do with slight variations. And you have to do that, otherwise*

mentally you wouldn't be able to get through the day. But when you want to do something new you have to apply the physics approach. Physics has really figured out how to discover new things that are counterintuitive, like quantum mechanics, so I think that's an important thing to do.[1]

Innovation improves the world and makes it worse. Using the laws of thermodynamics and economics we can understand innovation better. Economics teaches us about people, and thermodynamics teaches us about nature. Analyzing innovation through first principles teaches us new truths about the disorder it creates and why infinite innovation is possible.

Reasoning by Analogy

Analogy is our best guide in all philosophical investigations; and all discoveries, which were not made by mere accident, have been made by the help of it.

— Joseph Priestley, *a pioneer in chemistry and electricity*

Reasoning by analogy is learning from what others have done and are currently doing. You don't always have to figure things out on your own. Many times you can look around and see how others approach a similar situation and imitate it. Let me give you an example.

When my oldest son was one year old, he was still trying to figure out walking. He would pull himself up to my oval coffee table and while holding on with one hand would circle the table like a NASCAR driver. What stopped him from walking was he couldn't figure out how to stand up on his own. He always needed a piece of furniture to stand up, and he would never let go to venture off on his own. One day, I was with my son during a play date with a little boy who was a few months older and had already figured out walking. My son saw how this kid used his hands to push himself up and stand up on his own. Immediately, my son imitated his friend and stood up on his own and from that moment on was walking independently.

Learning from others' behavior is powerful, and we do it every day. We start as soon as we are born, with skills such as walking and talking. We have tools, agriculture, language, memory, technology, science, religion, literature, drama, and visual arts because we imitate each other. In fact, all elements of culture come from imitating each other. We do it when we are in any social situation by looking at each other. The way we dress, the places we choose to live, our profession, the places we work, and on and on.

This way of thinking and behaving makes things easier. You know that the things other people are already doing are possible because they are already doing them. When you see people doing something it also validates it as useful and desirable. A reliable way to influence others is to provide "social proof," a psychological phenomenon where people assume the actions of others in an attempt to reflect correct behavior for a given situation.

Reasoning by analogy has some limitations. If you want to improve upon something using reasoning by analogy, then you can only iterate based on things that exist, which is especially problematic for innovation because the way the world or universe works can be counterintuitive and difficult to understand. If you only look at what other people are doing or working on, then you can't discover secrets to unlocking the possible but unknown. The result is, you can't solve new problems precisely because they are not already solved.

Another limitation of reasoning by analogy is that you can't stop wanting what other people want. Humans excel when we learn from and imitate each other, but one thing we also learn is to want the things that other people want. We want these things, not because we need them, but because other people want them. René Girard called this mimetic theory. We begin to compete, hate, and commit acts of violence because we all desire the same thing. The desire to fight is problematic when innovating because you will feel pressured to play the same games other people are playing. You can argue about the need to compete or the value of fighting, and it may be necessary in the game you are playing. But, this is a limitation of reasoning by analogy, because instead of creating more opportunities you will fight over what opportunities already exist.

Finally, using reasoning by analogy, your individual results will vary. Deciphering what you can replicate and what was unique about someone else's circumstance is often impossible. Since everyone else's experiences seem unique, many people have concluded the outcomes cannot be known or planned and that the results are random or subject to "luck."

What can you learn from the founders of Facebook and Microsoft? Can you copy their success and build an operating system or a social network? Or can any of their experiences be systematized, or replicated in all circumstances? There are commonalities between Mark Zuckerberg and Bill Gates. Both founders attended Harvard and dropped out to pursue their successful startups. But what do you learn from their experiences? Is being accepted to Harvard and then dropping out a recipe for startup success? Of course not.

Be careful not to use reasoning by analogy as your only source of thinking, or you might conclude that the entire innovation process is random and chaotic and the only way to win is through luck. If you begin to rely on luck, you will almost assuredly fail. You will stop planning; you won't create a clear strategy and perhaps will rely entirely on pivots and iterations because you have convinced yourself that the future is unknowable.

Reasoning by First Principles

Reasoning by first principles is a way of thinking that can solve all the limitations of reasoning by analogy.

First principles are things you are sure are true. First principles are attributes so fundamental to something that their loss means that thing loses its identity.

Aristotle said that a first principle is the "first basis from which a thing is known"[2] and that pursuing first principles is the key to making any systematic inquiry. In physics, a calculation is said to be from first principles if it starts directly at the level of an established law of physics.

Tesla Inc. is an electric car company that has relied on reasoning by first principles to solve innovation problems. Tesla is the first American car company to go public since Ford Motor Co. in 1956. Large corporations in century-old industries and startups creating technologies that will mold the future can learn from Tesla because Tesla is both. Elon Musk, CEO of Tesla, revealed his approach to batteries, a core component to Tesla's electric cars. Batteries historically cost around $600 per kilowatt hour, but the basic materials cost eighty dollars per kilowatt hour. Instead of accepting the market price, Musk reduced cells to the things he knows to be true, in other words, batteries' first principles. Cells contain cobalt, nickel, aluminum, carbon, some polymers for separation, and a seal can. These items only cost eighty dollars. As Elon said: "So clearly you just need to think of clever ways to take those materials and combine them into the shape of a battery cell and you can have batteries that are much, much cheaper than anyone realizes."[3]

When you approach problems from first principles, you can uncover hidden solutions. Peter Thiel, the co-founder of PayPal and Palantir, the first investor in Facebook and a venture capitalist at Founders Fund, calls these hidden things secrets. "There are two kinds of secrets: secrets of nature and secrets about people. Natural secrets exist all around us; to find them, one must study some undiscovered aspect of the physical world. Secrets about people are different: they are things that people don't know about themselves or things they hide because they don't want others to know."[4]

As you try to uncover more challenging and more important secrets, reasoning by first principles becomes more critical because it is the only way you can understand them. Brothers Orville and Wilbur Wright emerged as inventors of the airplane at a time when others copied the flapping wings of birds to see if they could make a flying machine. These visionaries reasoned by analogy that the way to build an airplane is to imitate bird flight. The Wright brothers and others iterated their aircraft designs and came to understand flight principles enough to test various wing designs to achieve flight. No flapping was involved, as we now know. But this iterative and guesswork approach doesn't work for more advanced trips, like reaching the moon, Mars, or Pluto. We had to have a firm understanding of aerodynamics and flight to fly higher and faster than birds. Reasoning by first principles is the only way to discover these secrets.

The problem with first principles is it takes a lot more time and effort. It is so much easier to look around at methods and practices other people use, learn from them and copy them. Most people do not take the time nor do they have the inclination to define the issue, reduce it to its basic substance, and then reason up from there.

Secrets About People

There ain't no such thing as a free lunch.

I've interviewed hundreds of people and asked them to define innovation. Most people define innovation based on reasoning by analogy. They look at examples of innovation and use those models to create their definition. But for you, it is important to know how and why innovation works. To go further, we need to apply first principles to the innovation process itself. I have reduced innovation to two basic principles from economics and physics. Economics teaches us a secret about people and physics about nature. Once we understand a little more of these principles, we can define innovation.

Scarcity

Economic theory provides a deeper understanding of our world that will help us understand innovation. Scarcity is a basic observation in economics and drives innovation, capitalism, and human initiative. Even if you have never heard of scarcity before, you have certainly experienced it. It is the notion that there are never enough resources to satisfy human wants — not even one person's wants. My MBA class had an opportunity to visit Warren Buffett in Omaha, Nebraska. When I met the successful investor and chairman and CEO of Berkshire Hathaway, he was the richest man in the world. In 2017 his net worth was over $70 billion. During lunch, I sat across from Mr. Buffett and asked him if there was anything that he wanted but didn't have. At first, he told me "No." After he had thought for a moment, he said: "To be young."

I left that lunch realizing that I possessed the only thing that the richest man in the world wanted, but couldn't have. Your scarcity may be different from mine and Buffett's, but we all experience it. Scarcity means that neither you nor society can accomplish all of your goals at the same time. Scarcity causes constraints and limitations force us to prioritize.

Scarcity is eternal. It has existed, exists now, and will continue to exist regardless of any advanced state of technology we could develop. Scarcity forces decisions to allocate resources that maximize their usefulness, according to one's choices. Economists call this preference "utility," which is meant to express and measure the usability that an individual receives from a resource.

One way you express your personal preferences is how you choose to acquire and spend your money. Money is a way you can exchange a resource you have to obtain other resources. Perhaps you sell your time to an employer in exchange for money. You take that money and buy food, clothing, shelter, and other things. You express how much "utility" you get from something by what you buy with your money.

The things you buy have a price that is the result of scarcity and utility. The quantity people want (demand) determines the price and the amount available (supply). The more supply that is available, the lower the price. The less supply that is available, the higher the price. Demand works in the opposite direction compared to supply, the more demand there is, the higher the price. The less demand that there is, the lower the price. A market is a place where people agree on quantity and price. Market pricing is an efficient way to coordinate our priorities and the "utility" we individually and collectively receive from each resource.

When a price is high, it is because there is a high demand and a relatively small quantity available. A high price brings more sellers so supply increases. High prices can also alter the choice for buyers, lowering demand. Both or either of these changes will reduce the price.

Innovation is the process of reducing scarcity. Innovation changes the constraints to get more quantity from the needed resources, reduce the resources required, and satisfy more human wants. Innovation is the marginal improvement of scarcity.

Changing the constraints causes lower prices by increasing the quantity produced or higher prices by increasing the amount demanded. Innovation only refers to the modification of the current state, not the cumulative improvements. Therefore, all the innovation that has occurred and spread, up to the moment you are reading this, is baked into the system. All the prior innovation is now part of the given constraints, and we need something new to reduce our current scarcity.

Each side of an exchange gives up something scarce to receive something scarce in return. Because each side has different preferences, everyone is better off. The difference between what each side gives up and what it receives is value. Innovation creates value by increasing the difference between what is given up and what is received.

Secrets About Nature

> *The good thing about science is that it's true whether or not you believe in it.*
>
> — Neil deGrasse Tyson

Physics and thermodynamics hold a secret about life that is fundamental to our world and your understanding of innovation.

Thermodynamics

Thermodynamics deals with the relationships of energy. While I can't capture all the intricacies of the entire field, the three laws of thermodynamics contain the basic principles that you need to understand for our purposes. The first law states that you cannot get something for nothing because matter and energy cannot be created or destroyed. The second law says that disorder increases. You cannot return to the same energy state because there is always an increase in disorder and entropy. The third law states that entropy wouldn't increase if everything were completely disordered, but absolute disorder is unattainable.

Disorder

Thermodynamics calls the degree of disorder or randomness in a system entropy. Entropy is one truth that we are sure is true, and it will help you understand innovation and its effects.

Entropy is a gradual decline into disorder. It is one of the most important principles that weaves itself throughout life and a foundation for physics. We can feel entropy around us and have a lot of sayings in English that express this feeling such as, "shit happens," "life is what happens when you're making other plans," and "if you want to make God laugh, tell him about your plans." The French and Spanish have similar terms, and English speakers have appropriated them: "c'est la vie" and "asi es la vida."

The definition of order is "arranging things in a particular fashion" and disorder means "organizing things in disarray." Sean Carroll, a physicist at Caltech, helps nonphysicists like you and me understand entropy. "A nice organized system, like an unbroken egg or a neatly arranged pile of papers, has a low entropy; a disorganized system, like a broken egg or a scattered mess of papers, has a high entropy. Left to its own devices, entropy goes up as time passes."[5]

Increasing Disorder

Over time connected things move from a state of order to a state of disorder. In the grand scale of the universe, we see this happening as the sun's organized energy in the center of our solar system is scattered out in bits of light and heat across the universe. The sun, over the next billion years, will eventually burn out, its energy unevenly distributed throughout the cold and virtually empty universe.

We see this process happening in our personal lives, as well. Each time you ignite a combustion vehicle the engine converts the high energy gasoline in liquid form to an expanding gas that provides the energy to move our cars. The exhaust and the engine release swirling gas and heat into the air, in a much more disordered state than the liquid gasoline that just moments before was in a tank.

The tendency of things inside a system to change from order to disorder is officially known as the Second Law of Thermodynamics, that the entropy of an isolated system either remains constant or increases with time.

Systems

Thermodynamics divides the world, and the universe, into a set of connected things forming a whole it calls a system. Each system can be made up of subsystems, a self-contained system within a larger system.

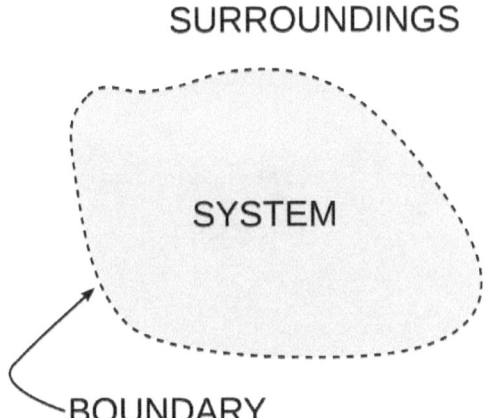

Our entire world is one system and there are many subsystems. As an example, the housing market in the United States is a subsystem. The things in this subsystem are connected to geographic location, the federal government, a banking system, currency, and citizens living in the boundaries of the US. The housing market in California is a subsystem of the real estate market in the United States. The housing market in San Diego is a subsystem of the real estate market in California. The housing market in North County San Diego is a subsystem of the real estate market in San Diego. Each of these subsystems is a set of connected things forming a whole and can be examined either together or as a whole.

Types of Systems

The Second Law of Thermodynamics states that entropy increases in an isolated system, a type that does not allow transfers in or out. But the law also describes two other entities: a closed system, which does not allow mass to transfer but does allow energy to move in or out, and an open system, which permits mass or energy to be gained or lost.

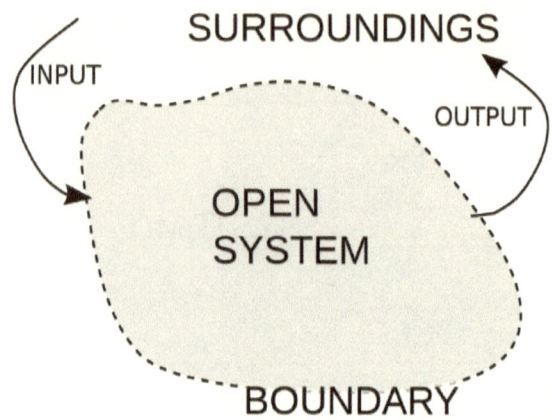

Isolated systems only increase disorder, because nothing can come in and create organization. With open systems, however, disorder can be reduced. Open systems can be influenced by other systems or things that reduce disorder. Total disorder will increase in some other fashion and in some other system. Disorder will always increase, so when an open system decreases its disorder, the result has to be disorder someplace else. Again, Sean Carroll, the physicist from CalTech, provides us with a practical explanation.

> *Not all systems are closed. The Second Law doesn't forbid decreases in entropy in open systems -- by putting in the work, you are able to tidy up your room, decreasing its entropy but still increasing the entropy of the whole universe (you make noise, burn calories, etc.). Nor is it in any way incompatible with evolution or complexity or any such thing.*[6]

Fortunately, many of our systems are open, which means that you can influence what happens and you can create order.

Infinite Innovation

Without understanding why something works, you can't explain why it fails. Now is the time to roll up the concepts of scarcity, supply and demand, pricing, entropy, order and disorder, and systems to help you understand innovation and its effects. Your goal is to understand the first principles of innovation so that you can manipulate the laws to your advantage.

Innovation Scarcity

Scarcity exists because of constraints, and innovation changes the constraints to reduce scarcity. Innovation does more with less. The benefit to understanding innovation in this way is to evaluate your idea better. What are the constraints you are changing? What is the scarcity you reduce? Are you able to save people time or money? Do you allow people to do something they couldn't do before?

Defining innovation as a reduction of scarcity allows you to do something you have never done before and rank innovation. Some approaches that change the constraints reduce scarcity more than others and some methods reduce scarcity less. You can take these different approaches and line them up based on how they reduce scarcity, and you have a continuum from small impact to large impact.

Based on this concept I developed the Innovation Rating System. There are six grades of innovation and not only does each grade have a different level of innovation, but each grade has a different effect on supply and demand and pricing. The six categories in ascending order: Trailing Industry Standard, Industry Standard, Leading Industry Standard, Mimetic (Imitation), The Wave, and Decade.

Innovation Systems

A system is a set of connected things forming a whole. Innovation happens in a system of connected things working to create and sustain innovation. Your system is most likely a startup. Your system is made up of a set of connected people who collaborate to accomplish a set of objectives or mission. A startup might be one of the best ways to cultivate innovation, but it is certainly not the only kind. A startup is a type of firm, but a firm can be one of many types of organizations, such as a for-profit company, a nonprofit, or a government.

A firm is a system that creates innovation and interacts with customers who use the solution. An industry is a collection of firms and customers. All of these systems are open.

Innovation Entropy

Startups are open systems where you can decrease entropy and create order. But based on what physics teaches us about entropy, open systems can create order, but disorder still increases inside and outside the system. You cannot avoid the effects. I call these phenomena the First and Second Laws of Innovation.

The first law is that innovation does not spontaneously occur. Just because open systems are capable of creating order doesn't mean that it will happen without effort. When people think of innovation they look at the progress civilization has made over the past one hundred years and assume that it will continue for the next thousand. It won't happen unless you make it happen.

The second law is that innovation creates disorder and entropy equal to the level of order the innovation creates. Its application to innovation helps you understand how you can create order, reduce scarcity, and manage the effects that flow from it. This law is critical to you because the speculative-graded innovations create a lot of order and reduce scarcity. The result of a high level of order is an equal amount of disorder.

As you look back in history, you can see the chaos created by significant innovations. Combustion engines changed the world for the better but also cause massive social investments in infrastructure, ongoing changes to labor and environmental laws, and damaging effects on the global environment that are almost uncontrollable. Nuclear energy is incredibly powerful and useful source of sustainable and clean energy. The disorder is evident in the effects of Hiroshima, Nagasaki, and Chernobyl. As a result of the risks of nuclear power, there are also significant global restrictions on the use and diffusion of the technology.

Disorder for potential innovations are also terrifying and can capture the public's imagination. Artificial intelligence has the potential to make humans immortal, and it also has the potential to lead to the extinction of the human race. Movies such as *The Terminator*, *The Matrix*, and *Ex Machina* represent the fear of the disorder that artificial intelligence can bring into the world if we are unable to manage it appropriately.

Many innovators ignore the resulting disorder because they are infatuated with the ability to overcome the constraints and the benefits of the innovation. Innovators who are focused on whether something is possible sometimes don't stop to think if they should proceed. Adopters, however, suffer directly from the disorder and struggle to manage it. Innovation's disorder will naturally suffocate the innovation unless you can sufficiently control the effects. Only when the chaos is in control can the innovation be firmly established as a lasting success.

The inventor Orville Wright lived to see his airplane invention used in two world wars but remained optimistic.

> *We dared to hope we had invented something that would bring lasting peace to the earth. But we were wrong.... No, I don't have any regrets about my part in the invention of the airplane, though no one could deplore more than I do the destruction it has caused. I feel about the airplane much the same as I do in regard to fire. That is I regret all the terrible damage caused by fire, but I think it is good for the human race that someone discovered how to start fires and that we have learned how to put fire to thousands of important uses.*[7]

Despite the inevitable damaging effects of innovations, the benefits of dramatic improvement will always push us forward. The Second Law of Innovation makes infinite innovation possible and unavoidable. Because of the chaos from the advances of those who came before us, you have no option but to continue to innovate. Infinite innovation creates unlimited economic growth potential.

Any problem you solve causes more problems to be solved, so you must continue the cycle because if you ever cease to improve, disorder will take over. Perfection, or a state of no change, never will be achievable, no matter how much you desire it. You do not want car crashes, plane crashes, hospital errors, and cockroaches in food. But, all of these are impossible. The best you can do is pursue enduring and persistent change.

Valuable Order

The system that creates order suffers internal disorder as a consequence, and the system receiving order suffers external disorder.

Innovation goes by too many restrictive names, like product and service or value proposition. These terms are restrictive because they refer to only one type of improvement. Innovation is generically called "valuable order" in the Second Law of Innovation because it is an arrangement of things in a particular fashion that is extremely useful or necessary to break previous constraints, and it is valuable because it reduces scarcity.

There are three types of innovation you can use to improve your core offering.
1. Performance: Improvements to products or services produced for external systems.
2. Funding: Process of acquiring resources to fund and sustain innovation.
3. Information Symmetry: Improving the product by accumulating and exploiting information or by collecting and disseminating previously inaccessible information.

Internal Disorder

Internal disorder is the damaging effect of innovation produced inside the system or firm that provides the valuable order. This disorder is equal to or greater than the amount of valuable order created.

There are five types of internal disorder you need to solve.
1. Core Process: Activities that produce the core offering.

2. Enabling Process: Activities that support the core process.
3. Economies of Scale: Marginal reduction of the costs of core and enabling process due to increased quantity.
4. Culture: Attitudes and behavior characteristics of members of the firm.
5. Governance: Process of controlling the organization.

Even though the amount of disorder created is equal to or greater than the order created, the cost of the disorder and the value of the order are not equal. The value of the order minus the long-term costs of the internal disorder is the net profit margin.

External Disorder

External disorder refers to problems the innovation creates inside the firm that incorporates the valuable order.

The organization that receives the innovation must introduce it into its system, and the disorder is equal to or greater than the amount of valuable order received.

Like internal disorder, even though the amount of external disorder is equal to or greater than the order created, the cost of the disorder and the value of the order are not equal. The value created is based on the preferences of the customers, and so the value they attribute can vary widely.

There are three types of external disorder.
1. Brand: Identity or image of a system.
2. Channel: Medium for communication and the passage of the core offering.
3. Network: A group of interconnected systems, people, or offerings.

Externalities

Externalities are positive or negative impacts to anyone not directly involved in producing or receiving the innovation. Since externalities affect those who do not participate directly in the transaction, the market does not price them into the innovation.

One example of innovation that produces externality costs is the automobile. Automobiles produced by the manufacturers and purchased by consumers do not include pricing to pay for the impact on the environment, road damage, accidents, congestion, and oil dependence. In a report published in 2011, the US Congressional Budget Office stated that "the public sector spent $146 billion to build, operate, and maintain highways in the United States."[8]

Each innovation that produces externality costs has to be approached individually.

Intro to The Gang

I want to bridge the gap between theory and how to apply it to your idea. To do this, I have created three composite personas who have separate ideas. Throughout the book I share conversation and analysis with you. After each chapter, we check in with the gang and they discuss how they apply the principles covered. The events, people, and quotes are fictitious. Any similarity to any idea is merely coincidental. The ideas are invented by me, but I have treated our discussions to show to you how to apply what you are reading to your own idea. At the end of the book I include each conversation in its totality so you can see how to analyze each idea, from beginning to end.

In advance of my first meeting, I ask each member of the gang to come prepared with the best idea and to have read Part 1 of *Without Luck*. Together we evaluate the ideas and help each team member understand the required strategic decisions.

The gang are all friends and join me in my office. Markus is a designer who wants to build an outsourced software development company, Sarah is an experienced manager who has an idea for an interviewing service, Joko is a software engineer who wants to leverage an audio algorithm he built in college to do something, but isn't sure about the best use.

Markus walks in and says "Hi," shakes my hand, and sits down in the chair on my left. Markus graduated from University of California San Diego with a degree in fine art, digital design. He is a product designer at a small startup but also takes on independent work. Markus has a full beard and is wearing an old faded light blue T-shirt with an image of the Marvel X-Men character Nightcrawler, dark blue skinny jeans, and a black pair of cap-toe oxfords without socks.

Joko is an Indonesian immigrant and a Stanford graduate with a dual degree in computer science and linguistics. He makes brief eye contact, smiles and sits down immediately in the chair on my right. As I get to know Joko better I realize that he is one the most intelligent people I have ever met. He is wearing a pair of light blue denim pants, a white long-sleeve button-up dress shirt, and a pair of black Nike running shoes. Joko works for a fast-growing company that recently held its initial public offering. It provides software to Fortune 500 companies.

Sarah walks in last. She smiles at me brightly, shakes my hand vigorously and says "Hi, David, great to finally meet you. Thanks for meeting with us today." I greet Sarah, and she sits in the middle chair, directly across from me. Sarah is dressed in a gray skirt, black flats, and a black long-sleeve shirt. Sarah has had a long career in technology, starting in 1996 with Netscape, after graduating from Wellesley College. She is currently data director of a startup helping news organizations generate sustainable membership-based revenue.

After some chitchat I jump-start the conversation. "I asked each of you to bring your best idea and to be prepared to discuss. Did you select your best and favorite idea? Markus, let's start with you. What is your favorite idea?"

Markus

> *I do a lot of consulting and contract to work as a designer, even though I have a full-time job. I turn away a lot of good business because I just don't have the time. I want to build an outsourced software development business. I want to work with people I like, clients I like, projects I like, and be able to take off when the surfing is good. I know that I can't do it on my own. I hate sales and business development. Most projects need developers. So, even though I need help with and managing the software developers I could build a good company. I know it wouldn't become a huge company, but I am 100 percent sure it could be a good company.*

Do you see a way that reasoning by analogy guided your idea?

> *Definitely. I have a friend that opened up a marketing and advertising agency a few years ago. He has over 100 employees, and he is making a lot of money. He has been able to craft the*

28

> *company culture as he wants. He loves what he does and is very successful. I turn away business every week, and I look at him and know that we could build something even better.*

Markus, have you used first principles in evaluating and planning your idea?

> *I have never thought about it this way. I think of my idea and the company I want to create as it relates to Maslow's hierarchy of needs. It is a theory of human motivation, represented by a pyramid. On the bottom of the pyramid are the most basic human needs, such as food, shelter, and clothes. As these requirements are fulfilled people want to feel safe, then belonging, self-esteem and self-respect, and eventually they will want to pursue self-actualization.*

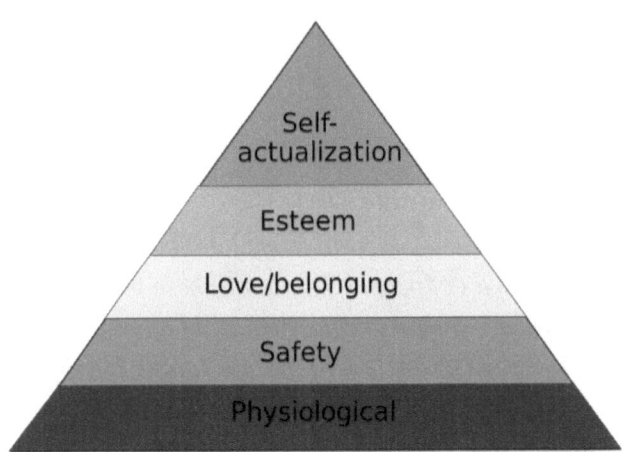

Maslow's Hierarchy of Needs[9]

> *This idea is critical to my idea and what I want for myself and for the people with whom I work. In fact, building this type of work environment is exciting. I have never worked at a place like that, and I think we could treat people like that and create a fantastic company.*

What problem do you want to solve?

> *Build good software.*

What constraints have prevented solving the problem?

There is more demand for skilled designers and developers than there is supply. For companies that develop their software, but where it isn't their primary line of business, it's hard to source and assess the talent of developers and designers.

What is your industry?

Consulting.

What is your "valuable order"?

A pool of shared and vetted professionals.

What do you expect is the most difficult "internal disorder" problem you need to solve?

Managing a consistent culture as we grow.

What do you expect is the most difficult "external disorder" problem you need to solve?

Keeping the brand strong and our interactions with customers.

Sarah

Sarah, what is your favorite idea?

I want to create a unicorn. In my job I have interviewed, hired, and fired a lot of people. Due to all these interviews, I am better at interviewing than anyone I know. I believe that I have passed on good people who looked great on paper but did not interview well. I always used to think that they just didn't live up to their claimed experience and education. Before I was offered the management role with my current company, I went out to dinner with several other partners in the business. All of the partners are related, and I would be the first in senior management not a part of their family. At dinner, the partners asked me several questions about my children and my relationship with my husband. The questions they asked me were different than any others I have had before. I did fine answering these issues, but it got me thinking back to the people I have interviewed and the potentially good people whom I didn't hire. Were they qualified and would have made good employees but they were just not good at interviews? How many people have I passed over, just because they were not good at interviewing?

So, I want to create an easy way for people to get the practice they desperately need. My idea is to have job seekers call in and interview with an experienced recruiter. The caller will receive a standard feedback form for each interview. As the job seeker calls in more, he gets more feedback and can track the progress. The caller pays a per-minute fee, and I add the charge to their phone bill.

I look at startups like Monster.com, Indeed.com, and LinkedIn. These companies built their businesses around job hunters, and I think it is a huge market with potential.

How has reasoning by analogy guided your idea?

Well, if I understand it correctly, I would say that the part about how I plan to charge. If I need to make someone sign up on the website and enter their credit card all before they call, then my conversion rates will be very low. So, I remembered the old 1-900 numbers that used to be used for phone sex. People would call the numbers and talk to a woman on the phone. The caller would pay a charge on their phone bill. So, I figured if people could just call my recruiters and we charge through their phone bill, then I get to avoid the entire sign-up and credit card process.

How have you used reasoning by first principles on your idea?

I have never heard of this before. I didn't use first principles. Well, maybe I didn't do it consciously, but perhaps I used the process without knowing it at the time. Can practice be reasoning by first principles? To improve anything people need to practice. I want to help people enhance their interviewing skills. So, this means that they need practice. My idea is just providing an easy way to for them to practice.

What problem do you want to solve?

I want to improve interviewees' interview skills.

What constraints have prevented solving the problem?

> *Job seeking is an occasional activity for interviewees, so the interview skills are under-developed. Companies have no incentive to provide training to a broad employee base. Recruiters usually work finding people for open positions, except for high-level positions.*

What is your industry?

> *Job searching and recruiting.*

What is your "valuable order"?

> *Allow job searchers to quickly and inexpensively receive consistent interview feedback.*

What do you expect is the most difficult "internal disorder" problem you need to solve?

> *Sourcing skilled interviewers.*

What do you expect is the most difficult "external disorder" problem you need to solve?

> *Reaching job searchers at the right time.*

Joko

Joko, what is your favorite idea?

> *I have learned that the sound of a person's voice will tell me if he is saying something important — at least to him. For the past few years, I have been tinkering with some software that I started writing in college to help me study for my classes. I recorded the professors' lectures and combined them with the textbooks and the exam questions and the correct and incorrect answers. Over time my software has learned to suggest a study guide based on the materials the professors would talk about in their lectures, including the inflections in their voices, compared to the exam question and answers. The software suggests the most relevant sections from the textbooks and other reading materials. I have improved the algorithms over time, and several people started using the software to study and get better grades.*

> The software was helpful in school, and I think it must have a commercial application, even though I am not sure exactly what that use might be. For sure, it helps students in higher education. With the right tweaks, it could help the NSA filter through the data it collects to prevent the next terrorist attack. Maybe investors could use it to prevent the next Enron fraud by comparing the calls with management to all the financial disclosures. I am sure there are some other uses. Maybe my software could interpret verbal cues for a larger artificial intelligence system. Honestly, I am not sure what the best or future use will be.

Can you explain how reasoning by analogy has shaped your idea?

> There are many contributing factors, but one thing that helped inspire me was playing around with Apple's Siri. I liked that Siri could listen to a voice and appear to make sense of the question. Sometimes when Siri doesn't have an answer, it just does an Internet search. So, the first few versions of my software were able to capture what a professor said and query the readings and exams to match the text. Those first versions took me far, even though the secret sauce would come later when I started weighting based on the verbal emphasis.

How do you incorporate first principles in your planning?

> For me first principles are part of the algorithms I wrote to analyze the sound of a person's voice to tell me if he is saying something important. I broke down the voice by hertz and the pace of the speech compared to other examples of speech from that person. Only by using the basic principles of speech could I break it down to reveal the secrets of what the person who was speaking considers most important.

What problem do you want to solve?

> Being able to analyze human conversations to provide actionable insights hidden from human ears and recollection.

What constraints have prevented solving the problem?

> *The processing power and the connecting nuances in the voice to the meaning and relevant data.*

What is your industry?

> *Artificial intelligence.*

What is your "valuable order"?

> *Intelligent speech recognition and query of content related to the conversation.*

What do you expect is the most difficult "internal disorder" problem you need to solve?

> *How the software scales will be the most difficult problem. It will be hard to use the software to analyze increasingly complex conversations and increasingly less related content.*

What do you expect is the most difficult "external disorder" problem you need to solve?

> *I think the biggest problem will be the network we connect to, meaning what we connect to other data, other systems, or with other artificial intelligence providers.*

PART 2: INNOVATION GRADES

The Innovation Rating System resembles the bond credit rating system. Capital markets rate loans (bonds) as an indicator of the likelihood of repayment. When a borrower is more likely to pay the interest payments and return the principal, the bonds receive a higher quality rating. Investors consider lower quality bonds speculative because the borrower is less likely to make timely payments. Bond grades help markets price bonds appropriately. High quality bonds earn less because investors are more likely to get all their money back. Lower quality bonds are priced to earn a lot more because sometimes investors will lose all their investment.

Until now there has not been a rating system to evaluate the quality of innovations, so project selection varies widely. The author David Graeber was able to capture perhaps too perfectly an all-too-common approach to assessing ideas. Graeber is an anthropologist at London School of Economics, and he wrote *The Utopia of Rules: On Technology, Stupidity, and the Secret Joys of Bureaucracy.*

> *Most people who work in corporations or academia have witnessed something like the following: A number of engineers are sitting together in a room, bouncing ideas off each other. Out of the discussion emerges a new concept that seems promising. Then some laptop-wielding person in the corner, having performed a quick Google search, announces that this "new" idea is, in fact, an old one; it —or at least something vaguely similar—has already been tried. Either it failed, or it succeeded. If it failed, then no manager who wants to keep his or her job will approve spending money trying to revive it. If it succeeded, then it's patented and entry to the market is presumed to be unattainable.*[10]

For the past thirty years, you have only had access to two recognized grades of innovation and both were defined by Clayton Christensen, the

Harvard Business School professor and author of "The Innovator's Dilemma," who coined the terms "sustaining" and "disruptive" innovations. Christensen defines sustaining innovations as improvements in products at the higher tiers of their markets where "they can charge higher prices to their most demanding and sophisticated customers, resulting in greater profitability."[11] Christensen defines disruptive innovation, as a "process by which a product or service takes root initially in simple applications at the bottom of a market and then relentlessly moves up market, eventually displacing established competitors."

The Innovation Rating System provides six grades, each with different benefits and risks. The more speculative grades are more valuable to society, and they have the potential to produce more wealth than lower grades. However, more speculative grades also carry more risks and create more market disruption, so they are less likely to be successful than prime grades.

The character of the improvements and the resulting disorder naturally dictate the innovation spectrum. This connection of improvements and disorder creates an inverse relationship between the higher grades and the likelihood of success. The more significant the innovation, the greater the resulting disorder. More significant disorder creates more risks that can prevent the innovation from becoming successful. However, if successful, speculative grades of innovation will have a greater impact on society than a lower level, produce an immense increase of wealth, and have longer staying power.

All other things being equal, you should select the project that has the highest level of innovation. But, that is like saying all other things being equal you should invest in companies with a higher rate of return and higher growth. Such statements or goals are self-evident but don't provide real guidance on how to distinguish between two otherwise equal projects with different outcomes.

Innovators like you have lacked a methodology to compare various projects. Without a language to communicate with each other clearly, your ability to collaborate is damaged. We can sometimes intuitively discern a good project from a bad one. But this blind approach means a lot of trial and error and an unacceptable failure rate. Lacking a methodology means our strategies may not align with the needs of the grade of innovation and it also means a lot of miscommunication and misunderstanding between teams, investors, and executives.

Innovation Rating System

The six innovation grades start with AAA, the lowest risk, and end with D, the highest risk. Each level has an inverse relationship to the quality and risks of the innovation. The innovation with the largest impact is Grade D, a speculative grade because it also carries to most risk.

The first four grades are reason by analogy innovations. These grades are Trailing Industry Standards, Industry Standards, Leading Industry Standards, and Mimetic. The other grades are reasoning by first principles innovations, Wave and Decade.

Every level faces six potential risks. High risk means the desired outcome is hard to predict and achieve. Low risk is the opposite, meaning achieving the result you want is likely. The innovation risks are:

- **Systemic & Industry**: general economic environment operations associated with a particular industry. A high systemic risk is a fast changing industry and worsening economic conditions. Favorable economic conditions and an industry resistant to change mean low risk.
- **Distribution**: supplying products and services through sales channels. When distribution risk is high, the channels are not well developed or getting access to the channels is difficult. When this risk is low, it is because the industry has an efficient and accepted process.
- **Competitive**: position relative to comparable industry options. High competitive risks are markets with many innovative players or a competitor with significant influence. Low risk occurs when there is no dominant player, and there are few innovative firms.

- **Team**: needed skills, correct decisions, and the right timing. High team risk is when uncertainty causes ambiguity about what skills are required to achieve desired outcomes. Low risk is when the skills for producing the results are predictable, or the process can be automated.
- **Financial & Technology**: achieving needed funding and ability to improve technology within a defined time frame. High financial and technological risk is when improvements may be impossible or the time horizon is hard to predict or otherwise discourages financial investments. Low risk is when the there is a proven approach with predictable outcomes.
- **Regulatory**: change in regulations and laws due to disruption. High regulatory risks are when the innovation is guaranteed to cause a change in government regulations. Low risks occur when laws exist to address the technology.

Below is a chart of the Innovation Rating System:

Rating-Grade	Type of Innovation	Risks	Guiding Questions
AAA	Trailing Industry Standards	Systemic & Industry	Is now the right time?
AA	Industry Standards	Distribution and AAA risks.	Do you have a way not just to create but deliver your product?
A	Leading Industry Standards	Competition and AA risks.	Will your market position be defensible 10 and 20 years into the future?
B	Mimetic	Team and A risks.	Do you have the right team?
C	Wave	Financial & Technology and B risks.	Is it possible to be profitable while providing the solution? Have you identified an opportunity others don't see?
D	Decade	Regulatory and C risks.	Can you create a 10x improvement with no close substitute?

Grades AAA, AA, A

If everyone agrees right up front that whatever you are doing makes total sense, it probably isn't a new and radical enough idea to justify a new company.

—Marc Andreessen

The three A grades attract attention because opportunities abound. The tension between these three grades is a lot of market opportunities at the bottom and bigger margins at the top, a classic supply and demand problem. Grade AAA has many customers compared to Grade A, which has fewer customers but higher margins. Grade AA has higher margins and fewer customers than Grade AAA, but more customers and lower margins than Grade A.

People generally like having more money than less money, so higher margins encourage firms toward Grade A. Not all firms can operate at Grade A because industry customers hold them back. Grade A does not have broad industry demand. Grade AAA and Grade AA have the most market opportunities because prices and margins are lower and attractive to buyers. Grade AAA attracts customers who are slower to adopt the innovation.

Below is a chart highlighting the differences between AAA, AA, and A.

AAA	AA	A
Zero Economic Profit	Low Margins	High Margins
Homogenous	Differentiated	Customized
Market Takers	Market Followers	Market Leaders
Perfect Competition	Monopolistic Competition	Oligopoly
Most buyers	Many buyers	Few buyers
Lower Quality	Standard Quality	Superior Quality
Proven effective in addressing common problems	Effective in addressing common problems	Suggested effective in addressing a common problem
Proven effective in many organizations and contexts	Effective in a few organizations and contexts	Successful in one or more organizations and contexts
Replication on a broad scale	Replication on a limited scale	Potential for replication

Grade AAA Trailing Industry

Grade AAA is lower quality than the industry standard. These practices are behind current industry practices and can benefit from benchmarking to industry standards. Trailing industry standards are effective because they have been proven to work.

Trailing the industry standard sounds like a dangerous place to be, but it isn't necessarily true. The only risk for Grade AAA is Systemic & Industry, which are the risks of general economic environment and risks associated with the operations of that particular industry. If the industry is fast changing or the economic conditions are worsening, then Grade AAA will become dangerous, especially in the short-term. If the industry is resistant to change and there are favorable economic circumstances, then Grade AAA can be a viable medium-term or long-term option.

Grade AAA has low exposure to the other five risk areas. Distribution risk is small because the industry has an efficient and accepted process. Competitive risk is low because the dominant innovative players are operating at Grade A. Team risk and financial and technology risks are low because the decisions are predictable and the small margins mean players can't afford technologic investments. Regulatory risks are low as long as the firm operates under the existing regulations.

Grade AAA can be a safe short-term option for incumbents. Opportunities exist for entrants, but there is usually no differentiation at this level. The guiding question for Grade AAA: Is now the right time to start your particular business?

Grade AA Industry Standard

Grade AA is the commonly accepted industry level of quality. This grade consistently delivers good results over other options and the industry has accepted this grade as the standard. Many organizations use the industry standard and it is very safe. It is the standard because you can expect it to work in many contexts.

Grade AA's primary risk is Distribution, supplying products and services through sales channels. When distribution risk is high, the industry does not have an efficient or accepted process. When this risk is low, it is because the industry has an efficient and acceptable process.

Grade AA has the same Systemic & Industry risks as Grade AAA, but all the other risks are low. Competitive risk is low because the dominant innovative players fight for Grade A margins. Team risk and Financial/Technology risk are low because the standard is defined and the decisions are predictable. Regulatory risks continue to be low as long as the firm follows the existing regulations.

It is better to be an incumbent than an entrant in Grade AA, but entrants can still be successful. The guiding question you need to ask: Do you have a way not just to create but to deliver your product?

Grade A Leading Industry

Leading Industry is a superior level of quality and is often called incremental innovation. Incremental innovation creates an improved version on the same terms. "On the same terms" means the normal way the industry defines performance. Grade A precedes a change in the industry standard. As more of the industry adopts the leading grade, over time the incremental innovation becomes the industry standard.

Organizations that are leaders look for the very best in any industry and any country. These practices have worked within one organization and show promise during early stages for becoming a best practice with long-term sustainable impact.

Grade A has the same Systemic & Industry and Distribution risk as Grades AAA and AA. Grade A also has competitive risk because all the participants are opposing each other in a search for higher margins. Competitive risk is losing position to comparable industry options. Industries with high competitive risks have markets with many innovative players or one dominant firm. Industries with low competitive risks have markets that lack a dominant firm, and have few innovative players.

The other potential risks remain low from Grade A. Team risk and Financial/Technology risk are low because the innovation occurs on the same terms and decisions are still predictable. Regulatory risks continue to be low as long as the firm operates following the existing regulations.

Incumbents love Grade A, as they should because they are relatively good at developing and distributing incremental innovation. Entrants are attracted to Grade A too because they see the opportunities, but Grade A is the worst place for them to start because they have to compete and create a distribution from scratch and are thus disadvantaged competing against Incumbents. Incumbents and their distribution channels are better positioned in a competitive environment. Without a channel in a competitive space, you should move to Grade AA or Grade B.

The guiding question for Grade AA: Will your market position be defensible 10 and 20 years into the future?

The Gang Analyzes Grades AAA, AA, A

I worked with the team to understand and define Grades AAA, AA, and A for their industries. After extensive discussions, each team member summarizes his understanding.

Markus: Outsourced Development

Define AAA grade for your industry.

I think Grade AAA for my industry would be what I am doing now. I do one-off projects for clients, on my own with no standard process. I do whatever the client wants. However they want it. The result sometimes is an inconsistent deliverable.

Is now the right time?

Marc Andreessen has said that software is eating the world, meaning that software will disrupt every market. So I believe that software development is and will continue to be an important part of any organization's operations.

Define AA grade for your industry.

Grade AA is small development shops that work with their clients to understand what they need and then contract with foreign developers to implement the design and build the software.

Do you have a way not just to create but deliver your product?

These companies require a robust sales process to be able to identify and close these business opportunities. There is an industry process for this; I think that with this team we could sell a lot.

Define A grade for your industry.

Grade A is the best tech companies. These companies, such as Google and Facebook, are leading software development regarding quality and speed. And for design IDEO is leading the industry. Competition for talent is fierce.

Will your market position be defensible 10 and 20 years into the future?

These leading companies can offer a lot of money, stock options, and career-boosting experience to engineers and designers. Competing with these companies is tough. So, I am not sure how I can compete with them. I might not have a defensible position, but they do.

Sarah: Interviewing Service

Define AAA grade for your industry.

Trailing industry standards is self-study on how to find a job and improve interviewing skills. Many job seekers read articles online or buy a book.

Is now the right time?

Job search industry mirrors the general economy. When the economy is strong, people feel more confident and are more likely to change jobs. When the economy is weak, people are more scared and usually stay with a job they have. I think things are stable now.

Define AA grade for your industry.

Recruiters are the industry standard. The hiring company announces or contracts with a recruiter who then finds candidates and prescreens them. Recruiters select the candidates they would like to present and prepare the candidates for the interviews with additional information regarding the client and the position.

Do you have a way not just to create but deliver your product?

I can deliver the services through the phones, which is a big part of the service. I would look to how companies attract new hires and advertise through the same channels, the Internet, recruiters, job fairs, and recruiters.

Define A grade for your industry.

I think this grade is the personal consultants helping provide customized advice and support to job seekers. These can be very expensive and are usually only for executives. There are not very many open positions, relatively, so competition for those

> jobs is intense, and the margins for the consultants can be very high because they are like professional sports agents.

Will your market position be defensible 10 and 20 years into the future?

> It might not be. This question highlights that my idea is a feature and a foundation of a business, but it is incomplete to sustain. If the idea is successful, it would likely mean that we will have to diversify and become involved in industry standard services, such as job placements or temporary staffing.

Joko: Audio Algorithm

Define AAA grade for your industry.

> For my idea, Grade AAA standards are basic transcription services or software. Radiology uses transcription to convert the physicians' verbal diagnosis from MRIs and x-rays to text that ends up in a patient record. This technology just changes the audio to text. Several companies provide transcription software. For the past few years radiology reimbursements have been getting cut, so I know that declining revenue has put stress on software providers in that sector.

Is now the right time?

> It is. We are at a time when we have enough processing power and Internet bandwidth to begin, and we can expect capacity to improve to meet our needs in the future.

Define AA grade for your industry.

> Grade AA now is software designed to take basic human interactions and respond with preprogrammed answers. I think of it like calling into a phone system for a credit card company. Software routes your call through the limited voice prompted options, such as "make a payment" or "customer service."

Do you have a way not just to create but deliver your product?

> The distribution process for Grade AA kind of business to business software is expensive and time-consuming. I think there is a way to evolve by focusing on some consumer services that

49

employees bring into the enterprise. Some startups like Box and Dropbox that have figured out how to make that transition.

Define A grade for your industry.

The difference between Grade AA and Grade A is pretty big. Grade A is Apple's Siri, Amazon's Echo, and Google's Home. This software is the current leading industry standard for voice recognition. The competition here is very intense. Apple, Amazon, and Google are all competing. Each of these three companies is growing quickly, has existing distribution channels, and can practically dedicate whatever resources they require to develop the technology.

Will your market position be defensible 10 and 20 years into the future?

If my technology remains static then it won't be sustainable because others will be able to replicate the functionality. The market position could be defensible if my technology continues to improve and we can dominate a niche before others can catch up.

Grade B—Mimetic

Grade B is a deliberate imitation of a behavior or practice from outside the native industry. This imitation can come from one of three areas: other industries, foreign countries, or nature. Many innovators see what works in one of those places and adapt the practice in a novel way for the native industry.

Imitating Other Industries

Innovators from one industry can succeed by adopting the practices from another industry. The practice could be a proprietary way an industry approaches a problem, or it could be the way it applies technology available to anyone.

It has been over thirty years since Apple launched the Macintosh personal computer, but only recently has healthcare in the United States learned to adapt the benefits that other industries have gained from the widespread use of computers. In 2001 only 18 percent of office-based physicians used an electronic health record (EHR) system. By 2013, adoption of EHR systems rose to 78 percent, in part because of a government mandate.[12]

Other industries adopted computers quickly. In 1987, the derivatives industry turned to electronic trading. CME Group is the world's leading and most diverse derivatives marketplace, handling 3 billion contracts worth approximately $1 quadrillion annually. The company is a marketplace for buyers and sellers that need to manage risk or that want to profit by accepting a risk.[13]

In 1987 the CME initiated the development of CME Globex platform and by 1992 began handling the first electronic futures trades. CME Globex provides users around the world with virtually 24-hour access to global markets and by 2016 managed 80 percent of trading volume.[14]

Imitating Foreign Countries

Innovators in one country can imitate practices from around the world. China, for example, has tech companies that resemble American companies; Baidu is similar to Google, Alibaba to Amazon, and DiDi Chuxing to Uber. You don't have to invent something if you can import successful innovations from other countries.

In many developed countries, telephony adoption started with landlines, which required significant infrastructure investments. In the past twenty years, many developing countries saw the adoption of cell phones in developed countries and decided they could skip the expensive landline investment and provide universal access to telephony via mobile phones. In Kenya, for example, 82 percent of adults have a cell phone. In China, 95 percent of the population has a mobile phone.[15]

Imitating Nature

Biomimicry is the "imitation of the models, systems, and elements of nature for the purpose of solving complex human problems."[16] Nature has spent billions of years on research and development and has already solved many of the problems we have created for ourselves. Many animals, plants, and microbes that surround us contain innovative secrets.

A modern example of biomimicry occurred with the Japanese bullet train. Residents who lived near rail tunnels complained of the sonic boom the bullet train created when emerging from the tunnels. The designer working to eliminate the noise turned to the kingfisher for answers. The bird dives through the air into the water to fish and has a unique beak shape that the designer copied. The redesigned nose of the bullet train reduced the boom to a muffled roar, and the train is also more energy efficient.

Mimetic Risks

Grade B has the same Systemic & Industry, Distribution, and Competition risks as all the A Grades. Team risk is high for Grade B because failure to execute well on any one of the issues is more punishing than in the other grades. It requires a new skill or experience to be able to cross multiple domains. Applying what has worked well in e-commerce to the healthcare industry, for example, requires an understanding of both disciplines. Team risk means the failure rate rises without the needed skill, correct decision making, and right timing. High team risk is when uncertainty causes ambiguity about what is even required to achieve desired outcomes. Low risk is when the approach for producing the outcome is straightforward, such as with Grades AAA, AA, and A.

The other innovation risks remain low for Grade B. Financial/Technology risk is low because the technology and financial models have been proved in different domains. Regulatory risks remain low as long as the firm follows existing laws.

The advantage of innovation by imitation is that many things have already been proved. Grade B is a safe place for entrants because they can leverage the work of others and apply it in a new context. Team risk is so significant because it requires industry experience to discern if the industry is ready and willing to accept the innovation.

Incumbents' focus is usually on Grades AAA, AA, and A and innovative incumbents are focused on capturing margins in Grade A. Often incumbents don't have access to innovations that occur outside their industry. Even if the incumbent is aware, it's hard to operationalize Grade B.

Incumbents can respond to Grade B in one of two ways. First, they can continue to look externally and innovate from imitation. This option creates a dilemma. Incumbents need a team that is capable of identifying the benefits of the innovation and also understands the native industry. However, to organize the team, the incumbent has to know what it intends to imitate, which it can't identify without the right team.

The second option for an incumbent is waiting until the mimetic innovation has some level of success in the native industry. Once this occurs, the incumbent must move quickly to respond and help make the innovation common, by building its proprietary technology or by acquiring the Grade B innovation. Once the industry begins to accept the practice, a larger and stronger incumbent has more power through its already existing distribution channels.

The guiding question for Grade B: Do you have the right team?

The Gang Analyzes Grade B

Markus: Outsourced Development

Define B grade for your industry.

> *I look at other industries and the way that they operate internally. We can learn from the way law firms are structured with partners and associates. An associate is hired out of law school and has a career pathway from day one. Over time they gain more experience and increase their professional network. They are managed by a partner who is responsible for the book of business and quality control of the services. Each partner is kind of a mini-company inside the firm. Many software firms break out and are small companies, or they are organized around middle managers.*

Do you have the right team?

> *I think I have the right team for where I am right now. But, if I implemented this type of structure, do I have someone who can architecture the structure? No. So, I would need to work with someone who knows very well the compensation structure, duties of the partners and associates, and the skill sets that define each position. Then, I would need to make sure that I maintain the vision so that additional hires are made in the right role and I could help associates progress to become partners.*

Sarah: Interviewing Service

Define B grade for your industry.

> *I think our industry could learn from online schools that allow remote access and instruction. There are important skill sets to communicating with resumes and interviewing, but there isn't an industry-leading way that teaches people how and what they should be doing. I could envision an online "school" that offers*

courses in resume building, networking, interviewing, and other valuable job searching skills.

Do you have the right team?

I don't have the right team to build a curriculum on job searching. I am missing someone who could help bridge the gap in creating courses that would instruct and assess progress. I would need someone from a school district or a university.

I do have the right team to build the service I envision. I think if we expand to standard recruiting and placement services then I would need an industry insider to bring on as a partner.

Joko: Audio Algorithm

Define B grade for your industry.

What artificial intelligence is trying to do is imitate nature. We are seeking to understand the neural networks and how they work so that we can recreate them with computers. There is a quote I like: "Any sufficiently advanced technology is indistinguishable from magic." Right now there is some "magic" that happens inside the brain. Eventually, we will understand how the technology works or replicate our design.

Do you have the right team?

There is a high team risk in artificial intelligence. I think that an engineering team is handicapped when approaching AI because they see learning as a design problem, primarily a mathematical equation. Some teams are involving neurologists now because they can provide some context to the way the brain develops. The way a child learns is understood by neuroscience, but it isn't the best way to teach a child. Have you ever met a neurologist? Would you want them to be a preschool teacher? Do you expect them to create a curriculum for a four-year-old? I have never met a neurologist that I would want to be a preschool teacher. Ask a preschool teacher how a child learns, and their perspective will be very different than a neurologist's perspective. So, when we are teaching computers how to learn perhaps the teams need to involve input from a variety of perspectives. Can a preschool teacher help an AI team create a curriculum for a computer based on their understanding of how a four-year-old child learns?

Grade C—The Wave

Clayton Christensen's work on Disruptive Innovation is the foundation for Grade C, which describes a process by which a product or service takes root initially in simple applications at the bottom of a market and then relentlessly moves up market, eventually displacing established competitors.[17]

To avoid confusing Grade C with the term "disruption" or market disruption, I have chosen to call this grade the Wave. The new technology starts at the bottom of the market, with a group that has historically gone without a solution. Over time the technology improves and swells, eventually leading the industry standard and serving high-end groups. The technology then crashes and becomes the industry standard.

When Christensen applied the term "disruption," he intended it to have a deliberate and precise meaning. Founders and innovators, however, use the word "disruption" to describe changes in industries as a result of any of the six grades, regardless of whether Christensen's theory applies. Peter Thiel, the PayPal co-founder, is critical of the term disruptive in his book *Zero to One:* "disruption has recently transmogrified into a self-congratulatory buzzword for anything posing as trendy and new."[18] Unfortunately, until now we have not had a vocabulary to express different types of innovation.

Christensen's initial theory was meant to help incumbents understand how they can dominate industries until an entrant comes along with an innovation and destroys them. Before Christensen's theory of disruption, many believed that incumbents were unable to respond because of their bureaucracies.[19]

While corporate bureaucracy prevents some incumbents from reacting to innovation, Christensen discovered that even well-run companies that are not handcuffed by bureaucracy do not respond well to Wave challenges. Christensen found that well-run incumbents ignore Wave innovations because in the beginning the Wave products are worse than the existing products and the margins for the Wave products are lower than the incumbent's current offerings. Christensen proposed that well-run companies don't pursue Wave opportunities because real customers don't want them and good management doesn't want to sell products that will make them less money. But Christensen proposed that Wave products are better than the current products in different ways and over time Wave products improve to compete on the same criteria. As Wave products improve, the entrants hold an advantage over the incumbent through an ability to operate profitably at the low end of the market. In other words, the newcomers can destroy the higher margins of the incumbents.

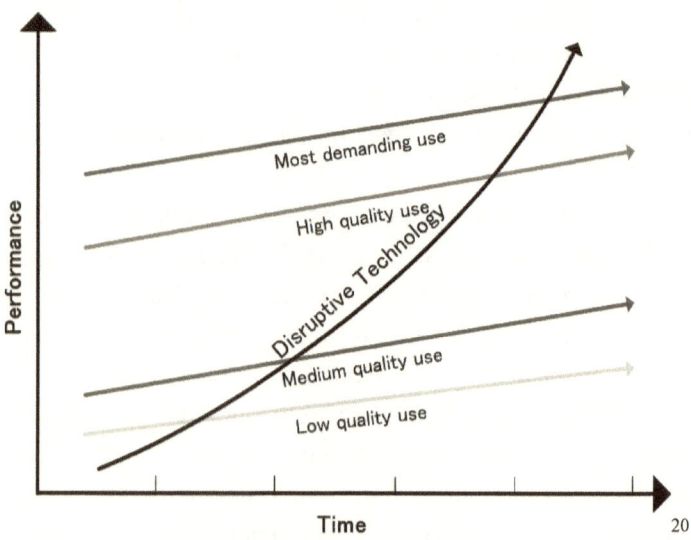

To be a Grade C innovation, the answers to all of these questions below need to be a resounding YES!
1. Is there a group that has historically been underfunded, understaffed, and as a result has gone without?
2. Is this group likely to appreciate lower cost "good enough" solutions?
3. Is it possible to be profitable while providing the solution?
4. Have you identified an opportunity others don't see?

Let's examine each question individually. Wave opportunities come in seeing an opportunity to help an underserved group.

1) Is there a group that has historically been underfunded, understaffed, and as a result has gone without?

This first part means the opportunity is often known in the industry and a solution already exists. However, the underserved groups can't access the solution because they are underfunded or understaffed. Your obvious approach is to look for a group that wants to buy the existing solution and create a way to deliver a cheaper alternative to that group. But, the secret you might miss is discovery of a group that currently hasn't even considered buying the existing solution. For example, individual households do not buy million dollar equipment to create and store their own electricity, because they cannot afford the equipment and utility companies take care of their power needs. But what if you could create a product that generates and stores electricity for individual households at a lower price than the households pay utility companies? The households are underfunded and therefore have been going without their own individual electricity storage.

2) Is this group likely to appreciate lower cost "good enough" solutions?

The heart of this question is whether the underserved group is willing to accept a solution that is worse than industry solutions, but still able to perform the job. This question does not imply a below industry standard solution. If you want to create a Wave innovation you cannot create a crappy product and just charge a lower price. The Wave solution is worse than the industry standard, but it is not made for the current industry customers, and it isn't made the same way the industry currently approaches the solution.

For example, if you provide energy storage equipment to utility companies, individual households don't want to buy the equipment. Conversely, if you provide energy storage to households, utility companies would not find the individual equipment "good enough." Individual households do not need industrial standards, therefore the solution for households can be worse compared to industry standards of the utility companies. No utility company would consider buying the household solution, even though it could meet the needs of households.

3) Is it possible to be profitable while providing these groups lower cost, good enough solutions?

This is perhaps the most difficult question. The answer is usually no, if you compete on the same terms. You generally can't do the same thing as the entire industry and charge a lower price over the long run. The economics of the solution is what makes the Wave so difficult and rare. You are most likely to be successful when the innovation itself makes the solution cheaper.

Since the underserved groups are going without a solution it means that the traditional distribution does not reach the underserved groups and the selling costs may be higher for the new entrant than for the current solutions in the market. You need to be careful, or else all the savings you generated on the product are eliminated in the increased distribution cost. Picking the right channel to deliver Grade C innovations is just as important as the solution itself.

Grade C has the same Systemic & Industry, Distribution, Competition, and Team risks as all the A Grades and B Grade. Additionally, Grade C has financial/technological risks because you might need outside funding while you are not profitable and your technology needs to improve in a reasonable time frame. High financial/technological risk occurs when improvements may be impossible or the time horizon is difficult to predict or otherwise discourages financial investments. Low risk occurs when you can take advantage of a proven approach with predictable outcomes.

Regulatory risk is the only remaining innovation risk that remains low as long as the firm operates in accordance with the existing regulations.

Choosing Grade C is attractive because, if you are successful, a new market segment opens and others cannot profitably compete. Over time, as your product improves and competes in the larger market, you retain the lower cost structure and new distribution channels and your solution moves like a wave, overtaking incumbents.

One mistake Grade C entrants make is attacking the broad market early as a low cost alternative. The larger market will pull you because there are customers that already pay more for a similar solution. You will think you can persuade the customers to switch. You will deceive yourself into thinking that since a "good enough" solution works for the underserved that the broad market will be content with the same solution. You will be mistaken because the Wave product is worse than what the existing customer already has and while there may be some exceptions, the low price is a warning sign, not a selling point.

Christensen has written about the degree to which incumbents should pursue Grade C innovations themselves. Christensen has never seen it work long term. In *The Innovators Solution,* Christensen and coauthor Michael Raynor wrote: "To our knowledge, no company has been able to build an engine of disruptive growth and keep it running and running."[21]

The Gang Analyzes Grade C

Here is a summary from our discussions on how our team applies Grade C to their ideas:

Markus: Outsourced Development

Is there a group that has historically been underfunded, understaffed, and as a result has gone without? Is this group likely to appreciate lower cost "good enough" solutions?

> *In my industry I think that the way outsourced software development has evolved includes some aspects of Grade C. Software development in the United States has been very expensive and required technical and management skills to be able to create effective software. As a result, many companies did not create customized software for their needs.*

Is it possible to be profitable while providing the solution?

> *Yes, by using developers with very different economic needs. Over the past few years, many consulting companies have partnered with overseas developers to lower the cost of software development. It is easy to be profitable even under the traditional model.*

Have you identified an opportunity others don't see?

> *I don't think I see anything special. Many people are adopting similar models. This discussion is helpful because innovators who can improve and maintain quality will be able to provide services to the whole market.*

Sarah: Interviewing Service

Is there a group that has historically been underfunded, understaffed, and as a result has gone without? Is this group likely to appreciate lower cost "good enough" solutions?

> *People entering the job market, such as the young and immigrants, are underserved. They have low resources and little experience. Recruiters can't do anything with them usually. High-end recruiters definitely can't do anything with them. So, they are left on their own not receiving any help.*

Is it possible to be profitable while providing the solution?

> *Maybe. If this is my strategy, to target the underserved, I would have to figure out if I can contract with professional interviewers while keeping my fees low enough. But, the most difficult challenge may be how to reach the customers. How I advertise and inform those underserved may be very expensive.*

Have you identified an opportunity others don't see?

> *I see a problem and an opportunity. What I don't know is if this underserved group sees value in the service.*

Joko: Audio Algorithm

Is there a group that has historically been underfunded, understaffed, and as a result has gone without? Is this group likely to appreciate lower cost "good enough" solutions?

> *Yes, the industry is still young, but students are usually underserved and do not have the resources for analytics, artificial intelligence, or speech analysis to help them study.*

Is it possible to be profitable while providing the solution?

> *I think so. The software is scalable and improves with more data. The distribution should be relatively inexpensive since we*

could target individual schools at a time and students live close to each other.

Have you identified an opportunity others don't see?

Well, no one else is pursuing the idea in this manner. Who wants to sell to students when this could be refined and sold to banks, Wall Street firms, hedge funds, and governments? But, I could start with students and then as the software improves I can move up market to the more lucrative opportunities.

Grade D—Decade

Peter Thiel described a type of innovation so far advanced that all customers switch to it. Thiel called this grade of innovation a "breakthrough,"— and defined it as something new or an improvement so significant "at least ten times better than its closest substitute in some important dimension to lead to a real monopolistic advantage." [22]

A 10x improvement refers to an order of magnitude improvement. Differences in order of magnitude can be measured on the logarithmic scale in "decades," or factors of ten, which is why Grade D is called "Decade." The word breakthrough can be interpreted as breaking a constraint. I have heard people use the term breakthrough when referring to a Grade A innovation. A decade innovation won't be confused with other types of innovation.

The above chart demonstrates the improvements needed for three decades. When the technology is primitive, a 10x improvement can be fairly basic. The next iteration needs to be 10x better than the most recent innovation, or 100x better than the primitive technology. The fourth Decade will be 10x better than the last, 100x better than the first innovation, and 1,000x better than the primitive technology. The invention of the horse carriage was a 10x improvement and the car 10x over the carriage, and the airplane a 10x improvement over the car. Achieving a 10x improvement over the airplane has so far proved more difficult.

Recent Decades are the founding of some of the world's most valuable companies. These companies have no close competitor and dominate a market. Google's search engine, Amazon's e-commerce and logistics, Facebook's social network, Apple's iPod and iTunes, and Microsoft's Office Suite and operating system. Other Decades have been created by the government and opened to the public, such as the Internet, and some are closely guarded and regulated, such as nuclear power.

Creating a Decade innovation is harder for incumbents because their focus is on executing well on an existing business. Decades are more likely to happen for you as a new entrant where you have the flexibility to identify how to overcome the critical technological or social constraints and achieve a monopolistic advantage. Even with such a significant advantage, you still must manage all the risks to achieve and sustain a monopoly.

Grade D accumulates all the innovation risks from all other grades: Systemic & Industry, Distribution, Competition, Team and Financial/Technological. Additionally, Grade D carries regulatory risks. High regulatory risks occur when the innovation is guaranteed to cause a change in government regulations. Low risks occur when existing laws address the technology.

Grade D's risk of regulation is a result of the Second Law of Innovation, which is that innovation creates disorder equal to the level of order the innovation creates. Grade D creates an enormous amount of order and value (10x), and the result is a huge amount of problems from the disorder (10x). Society has to manage these problems through regulation to protect the public, as in the case of the disorder created by the automobile: traffic laws, mandating car insurance and forcing users to receive and maintain a driver's license. Other Decade technologies are highly regulated, such as nuclear energy.

Sometimes the disorder problems are manifested in the effects of the monopoly. Companies with a monopoly have immense power in their markets, so their business decisions can be anti-competitive. In the late 1990s, Microsoft faced antitrust charges in the United States for the way it combined the Windows operating system and Internet Explorer web browser. In the 1990s Windows enjoyed a monopoly, with nearly 100 percent market share of desktop operating systems. Microsoft used its power to destroy a competitor and control the way millions of people access the Internet.

A little startup called Netscape launched a web browser and dominated the browser market in 1994, going public in 1995. Netscape was founded by Marc Andreessen, Jim Clark, and William Foss. Netscape charged forty-nine dollars for its browser and sales were booming until Microsoft released Internet Explorer for free and included the software with its Windows operating system. Bundling Internet Explorer essentially meant no one had to buy a browser for a personal computer. This anticompetitive behavior led the United States government to bring charges against Microsoft. When a breakthrough company becomes a monopoly, the result will always be incredible damage.

Other Decade companies have experienced similar problems. In 2016 Google was under threat of antitrust charges in the European Union for its mobile phone operating system, Android. In 2016 Facebook faced an antitrust investigation related to its privacy and advertising policies. In 2013 Apple was involved in an antitrust case and fined $450 million for attempting to fix the price of e-books.

Bruce Gibney is a Partner at Founders Fund and wrote in the company's manifesto that Decade Innovations, especially early in their life cycle, are not always popular, are difficult to assess, have surmountable technology risk, and if successful their technology will be extraordinarily valuable.[23]

Grade D innovations meet these criteria precisely because the advancement over other solutions is so pronounced. They are not popular because they cause significant problems, which often lead to regulation, but do not come with natural solutions. They are difficult to assess because the initial claims are likely outrageous. They have unique technology risks because the approach is novel, which is why the innovation has not been discovered previously. It is so valuable because it consumes everything that could be considered a substitute and therefore adoption can be extremely rapid.

Brian Singerman, a partner at Founders Fund, noted: "Regulators are not the enemy. There are reasons for the regulations to exist. The best entrepreneurs are the ones who can work well with engineers and with regulators. It takes a certain skill set to do that."[24]

Guiding question: Can you create a 10x improvement with no close substitute?

The Gang Analyzes Grade D

Here is a summary of our discussions on how our team members apply Grade D to their ideas:

Markus: Outsourced Development

Can you create a 10x improvement with no close substitute?
> *I am not sure what kind of innovation would be a 10x improvement. It would mean getting forty hours of software development in four hours, or keeping quality high and paying ten dollars to the one dollar for the costs. Not sure what could cause that to happen.*

Could your idea create or face any new regulations?
> *No.*

Sarah: Interviewing Service

Can you create a 10x improvement with no close substitute?
> *No, I don't see what a 10x solution would look like in this market. I don't think my idea is 10x better.*

Could your idea create or face any new regulations?

No.

Joko: Audio Algorithm

Can you create a 10x improvement with no close substitute?

Maybe. I think what I have built has no close substitute. It has a lot of potential, but there is a lot of work to do. Artificial Intelligence would certainly be a Decade innovation. It is not impossible and eventually someone will discover it. It is already not popular and some people want to prevent it and certainly there is already a fear of AI. But, AI will be the most valuable invention the world has seen. If it is created by a private individual, the invention will make them the richest person in the world—if they can avoid the regulation. I don't want to claim that I am creating AI, but layering what I have created can help the AI understand humans better.

Could your idea create or face any new regulations?

Yes. I don't know what the regulations should be, but AI will definitely face regulations.

Industry Application of the Six Grades

The energy industry is a good industry to analyze because it exhibits all six types of innovation. These types are listed below, including their percentage of total US electricity generation in 2014.
- Grade AAA, Trailing Industry Standards: Coal 39 percent
- Grade AA, Industry Standard: Natural Gas 27 percent
- Grade A, Leading Industry Standard: Renewables 13 percent
- Grade B, Mimetic: Solar Power 1 percent
- Grade C, Wave: Tesla Powerwall 0 percent
- Grade D, Decade: Nuclear Power 19 percent

Trailing Industry Standard: Coal

Coal is becoming Trailing Industry Standard. It is filthy to produce and to burn. Heavy metals and sulfur exist in the exhaust, so the burning is not clean. The emissions are 300-1,000 parts per million in nitrogen oxides (NOx) and carbon dioxide (CO_2). Nevertheless, coal produces a lot of energy in the United States. In 2014, coal was used to generate 39 percent of the 4 trillion kilowatt hours of electricity used in the United States.

Standard Energy: Natural Gas and Fossil Fuels

Natural gas is Industry Standard and generated 27 percent of electricity consumed in the US. Natural gas can burn much more efficiently and cleanly than coal. Recent technology can get emissions down into the 10-100 parts per million of NOx and CO_2.

In the United States shale gas will be a source of energy in the US for the next twenty years. There is so much natural gas in the US that gas pipelines have been turned around from net import to net export. Many energy companies are attempting to compress and liquefy the gas to sell it to emerging markets like China.

Leading Energy: Renewables

Renewable energy, such as wind, hydropower, and biomass, is Leading Industry Standards. Renewable energy produces roughly 13 percent of US electricity.

Electricity generated from wind turbines has increased significantly in the US since 1970 and provided about 4 percent of US electricity in 2014. Wind is tricky. It can be seasonal and usually only blows during the day, so it will never be a primary source.

Hydropower, the source of almost 6 percent of US electricity, is a process in which flowing water spins a turbine connected to a generator. Most hydropower is produced at large facilities built by the federal government, like the Grand Coulee Dam. The West has many of the biggest hydroelectric dams, but hydropower facilities operate around the country. Hydropower is unlikely to grow because of environmental impacts on habitat in rivers below dams and in areas behind the dams that become reservoirs.

Biomass is material derived from plants or animals and includes lumber and paper mill wastes, food scraps, grass, leaves, paper, and wood in municipal solid waste (garbage). Biomass is also derived from forestry and agricultural residues such as wood chips, corn cobs, and wheat straw. These materials can be burned directly in steam-electric power plants, or they can be converted to a gas that can be burned in steam generators, gas turbines, or internal combustion engine generators. Biomass accounted for about 2 percent of the electricity generated in the US in 2014.

Mimetic Energy: Solar Power

Solar power, or photovoltaics (PV), is an innovation imitating plants and organisms, like plankton, which generate their food from the sun through photosynthesis. Although the fuels produced by PV are different than photosynthesis, they are thermodynamically equivalent. PV and another method, called solar-thermal electric, are the two main types of technologies used to convert solar energy to electricity. PV conversion produces electricity directly from sunlight in a solar cell. Solar-thermal electric generators concentrate solar energy to heat a fluid and produce steam to drive turbines. In 2014, less than 1 percent of US electricity generation came from solar power.

Wave: Tesla Powerwall

Tesla Inc.'s Powerwall has the potential to be a Grade C innovation. The Powerwall, announced in April 2015, is a home battery that charges with electricity generated from solar panels, when utility rates are low, and powers the home in the evening, when rates are high. Combine solar panels and one or more home batteries, and Powerwall offers independence from the utility grid.

Tesla calls itself "not just an automotive company, [we are] an energy innovation company."[25] In the future it is more likely Tesla becomes an energy company that makes cars than remaining a car company that uses batteries.

A Wave product is worse than the currently available products when judged by traditional criteria, but better in different ways. The operators of the electric power grid are developing storage options to smooth out variances between production and use. The nascent energy storage products used by utility companies are better than Tesla's Powerwall at storing large quantities of energy, but Tesla's Powerwall is not an industrial product; it is for individual households.

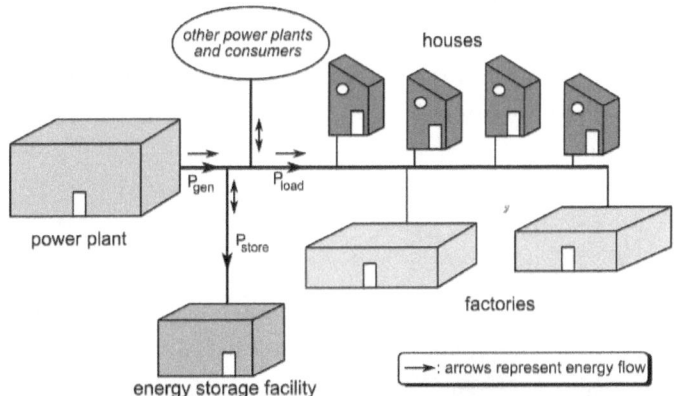

The answers to these three questions suggest that the Powerwall is a Grade C innovation.

1) Is there a group that has historically been underfunded, understaffed, and as a result has gone without?

While there are residential uses and demands for energy, storage is prohibitively expensive and only available to utilities, corporations, and the super-wealthy.

2) Is this group likely to appreciate lower cost "good enough" solutions?

Residential energy storage does not have the same requirements as grid energy storage. These two markets do not have the same problems and do not need the same solution. San Diego Gas & Electric, for example, is a regulated public utility that provides energy service to 3.5 million people through 1.4 million electric meters in the San Diego area. Its requirements are much different from a household of five people storing enough energy to power their home during the evening.

3) Is it possible to be profitable while providing these groups lower cost "good enough" solutions?

This is perhaps the most difficult question to answer from the outside. An ancient Chinese military approach to military strategy and tactics is addressed in the book *The Art of War*, attributed to Sun Tzu.

> *All men can see the tactics whereby I conquer, but what none can see is the strategy out of which victory is evolved. i.e., everybody can see superficially how a battle is won; what they cannot see is the long series of plans and combinations which have preceded the battle.*[26]

Each quarter Tesla's form 10-Q is available for public review, but not its strategy. Tesla is currently running at a loss, but the unit economics are good, and the answer to this question will play out of the coming years.

Decade: Nuclear

Nuclear energy is a Decade innovation that is burdened with regulation. Even though nuclear power will never take hold in the US, many European and Asian countries generate the majority of their power from nuclear energy with no plan to reduce reliance. Nuclear power was used to produce about 19 percent of all US electricity in 2014.

Nuclear power plants produce electricity with nuclear fission, such as radioactive decay, to create steam that spins a turbine to generate electricity. Nuclear power has one advantage over other nonrenewable energy technologies: It contributes little to global warming emissions. Since emissions are so low, an expansion of nuclear power would help address climate change.

However, this advantage must be weighed against the added risks to human health, the environment, and global security that nuclear power creates, as well as the nuclear industry's failure to show that it can operate cost effectively without the help of government subsidies. A serious accident at a nuclear power plant could release significant amounts of dangerous radiation, with disastrous consequences for the environment and an increased risk of cancer for those exposed to the radiation. Other security risks include both the risk of sabotage and terrorist attacks on nuclear power plants and the risk that nuclear materials will be stolen and used to create weapons.[27]

Introduction to Bond Ratings

This chapter on bond ratings is included to help you understand more about how innovation grades are structured. If you are already familiar with how bond ratings work, or if this sounds incredibly boring, you can skip this chapter. The important take away is how the bonds are rated and the qualities that impact ratings.

Bonds are evaluated by credit rating agencies such as Moody's, Standard & Poor's and Fitch. A bond is assigned a letter designation, such as AAA, B, or C, that represents its quality. A higher bond rating accounts for a higher likelihood of repayment, which is inversely related to the effective rate of return to the investor. A lower bond rating represents potentially higher return, but less likelihood of repayment.

Credit Risk and Analysis

A bond is a financial obligation of an entity that promises to pay a specified sum of money at specified future dates. The organization that pledges to make the payment is called the borrower or issuer of the security.

The investor who purchases a fixed income security is the lender or creditor. The payments that the issuer agrees to make at the specified dates consist of two components: interest and repayment of funds borrowed, which is called the principal.

Credit analysis of any entity—either a corporation, a municipality, or a sovereign government—involves the analysis of quantitative and qualitative factors over the past, present, and future. A credit rating is an indicator of the potential for default, which occurs when the issuer is unable to make the required payments on debt obligations. It represents in a simplistic way the credit rating agency's assessment of an issuer's ability to meet the payment of principal and interest.

While credit rating agencies will explore various aspects of the business, traditional credit analysis will consider the five C's of credit: character, capacity, capital, collateral, and conditions. Character refers to a borrower's reputation. A private equity company in search of higher return that has a history of loading up companies with debt and then defaulting in bankruptcy is considered differently than a founder with thirty years of steady growth. Capacity measures a borrower's ability to repay a loan by comparing free cash flow against obligations. A company generating strong cash flows from recurring revenue on long-term contracts is more favorable than a company with inconsistent and unpredictable revenue with high fixed costs. Capital is the amount the borrower contributes toward the investment or has available. Large contributions by the borrower or significant assets comparable to the debt will lessen the chance of default. Collateral is something that secures the loan. Typically, this is property or significant assets. Defaulting on debt with collateral, such as a building, substantially reduces the risks of unsecured debt. Finally, the conditions of the debt, such as the time frame for repayment, interest rate, and the amount of principal included in payments. A period of ten years is much riskier than two years, and an interest rate of 5 percent above prime is much more attractive to the lender than 1 percent above prime. All of these factors need to be weighed together.

The bond evaluation process begins when a rating agency receives a formal request from an entity planning to issue a bond in which it seeks a rating. The cost associated with obtaining a credit rating is paid by the entity making the request for a rating. A rating is sought because without it the issuer likely can't issue the bond. The rating assigned applies to the specific bond to be issued, not to the entity requesting the rating.

After a credit rating is assigned to a corporate debt obligation, a rating agency continues to observe the credit quality of the issuer and, as circumstances change, can reassign a different credit rating to its bonds. An "upgrade" occurs when the credit quality of an issue improves; a "downgrade" occurs when the credit quality of an issue deteriorates.

Typically, before an issue's rating is changed, the rating agency will announce that it is reviewing the bond with the potential for upgrade or downgrade. This process is called a "rating watch" or "credit watch." In the announcement, the rating agency discloses the direction of the potential change in rating—upgrade or downgrade. Typically, the analysis is complete and announced within three months.

S&P Short-Term Issue Credit Ratings [28]

Grade	Current Strength	Future Prospect
AAA Investment Grade	The issuer's capacity to meet its financial commitment on the obligation is strong.	
AA Investment Grade	The issuer's capacity to meet its financial commitment on the obligation is satisfactory.	An AA rating means the issuer is more susceptible to the adverse effects of changes in circumstances and economic conditions.
A Investment Grade	The issuer's capacity to meet its financial commitment on the obligation is adequate.	Adverse economic conditions or changing circumstances are more likely to lead to a weakened capacity of the issuer to meet its financial commitment on the obligation.
B Speculative	The issuer currently can meet its financial commitments.	The issuer faces major ongoing uncertainties that could lead to inadequate capacity to meet its financial commitments.
C Speculative	The issuer is currently vulnerable to nonpayment	Dependent upon favorable business, financial, and economic conditions for the issuer to meet its financial commitment on the obligation.
D Speculative	The issuer is in default or breach of a term.	Rating will be used upon the filing of a bankruptcy petition or the taking of a similar action and where default on an obligation is a virtual certainty.

PART 3: INNOVATION TYPES

Whenever people coordinate they must solve problems related to the characteristics of the product or service they provide, internal operations and distribution of the product or service. The Second Law of Innovation dictates that there is disorder equal to the valuable order and the disorder will occur within the coordinating group, called internal disorder, and outside the group, called external disorder. The product or service is the reason people collaborate and is the valuable order. From these categories spawn thirteen types of innovations.

Your choices are to select what grade of innovation you want to implement for each type of innovation. The categories and types are listed below and the next thirteen chapters explain what the types are, how to think about them using first principles, and guiding questions to help you decide and plan your approach.

First principles analysis can help you whether you are a beginner or an expert in each type. If you are starting your career you can use the first principles as a foundation to build your knowledge. If you already have significant experience then you can layer this analysis on top of what you already know for actionable insights.

Category 1: Valuable Order

1. Core Offering—Product or services produced for external systems.
2. Funding—Process of acquiring resources to fund innovation.
3. 3. Information—Improving the product by accumulating and exploiting information or by disseminating previously inaccessible information.

Category 2: External Disorder

4. Brand—Identity or image of a system.
5. Channel—Medium for communication and the passage of the core offering.

6. 6. Network—A group of interconnected systems, people, or offerings.

Category 3: Internal Disorder

7. Core Process—Activities that produce the core offering.
8. Enabling Process—Activities that support the core process.
9. Economies of Scale—Marginal reduction of the costs of core and enabling process due to increased quantity.
10. Culture—Attitudes and behavior characteristics of members of the firm.
11. 11. Governance—Process of controlling the firm.
12.

Category 4: Blends

13. Customer Service—Combining multiple types of innovation to influence customers in a particular manner.
14. Complex Coordination—Combining multiple types of innovation smoothly to create a sustainable advantage.

Products

> *Great companies are built on great products.*
> —Elon Musk

New products are celebrated and widely promoted through mass media, journalists cover product launches and write hero stories about the founders who develop new products. Founder stories whip a cult of personality until adoring fans give founders rock star or movie star status. The founder of Napster, Sean Parker, was even portrayed by Justin Timberlake, a rock star turned movie star in the blockbuster movie *The Social Network*. Even academics are captivated and isolate a product's commercial success as a single dimension measurement of a company's success or failure. Innovative products also attract competition in the industry to respond and release a similar product.

Products get so much attention because they are the most visible and easily understood innovation type. The other innovation types are not as public and are sometimes intentionally hidden to conceal strategy, but all other innovation types are dependent on and supportive of the product. Indeed, no organization can exist without an offering, so all activities in the organization support the product.

When buyers and sellers come together in a rational market, each side communicates with the other its priorities about scarcity. (Throughout this chapter I will refer to the offerings as just "products," meaning both products and services.) The buyer values the product more than money, and the seller values money more than the product. The market exchange works because both sides receive value, which I defined as receiving something that has more worth and is more scarce than the thing the buyer or seller trades away. Innovation increases the value of the exchange.

You are creating a product, so it is critical that you understand how the buyer assesses its value. The buyer is trying to manage her resources to reduce scarcity. To do this, the buyer either consumes a resource, using it up; invests in a resource, with the expectation that it will repay the cost; saves a resource, preventing waste; or insures the resource, to protect against loss.

Buyer Motivation: Consumption

The first buyer motivation to manage scarcity is to consume a resource to accomplish a useful activity. The reason why customers consume is that they enjoy the product.

Intrinsic motivation is when your reason is not to generate an outcome, which is a stark contrast to the other motivations. You just enjoy the thing. You can eat because you need to, or you can eat because the burger at your favorite restaurant tastes good. You can buy art because you think that it will be worth more in ten years or buy art because you like it. You can play video games as a way to connect with other people or because you enjoy the games. You can listen to modern music because you are afraid of being left out of current trends or because you like the music.

Buyer Motivation: Investment

Investment is the desire to leverage a resource with the expectation that the usefulness will repay more than the original cost.

In modern society, you have sophisticated investment options such as public stock markets, bond markets, derivatives, and various corporate structures. But there are also much more simple investment decisions, such as a landscaper deciding to purchase a truck to use in her business or a law firm hiring a new attorney.

Buyer Motivation: Saving

Saving means using a scarce resource to avoid or reduce the spending of other resources. A customer is looking to spend resources that will save money, time, talents, use of machines, or other valuable items.

Savings and investments can appear similar, but they are not the same thing. In your personal finances, you can generate ten dollars in extra monthly cash flow by investment or by savings. You can earn ten dollars in interest by investing $12,000 in a bank account that pays 1 percent annually. Alternatively, you can generate ten dollars in savings by deciding not to buy two cups of Starbucks' coffee. Savings means your trade-off is either to reduce consumption of coffee or to get coffee by some other means, such as the coffee provided for free at work. Investment also has a trade-off. To earn the ten dollars in interest every month, you cannot spend the $12,000 on other things.

Organizations often look for savings by reducing expenses or by avoiding future spending. For example, an information technology (IT) department could cycle out employees' computers for newer systems. The result could be avoiding the inevitable increase of support calls and reduce current support calls.

Buyer Motivation: Insurance

Insurance is the fourth type of motivation for a buyer. Many people are familiar with the concept of insurance through buying policies that protect against the risk of loss, such as health insurance, auto insurance, and life insurance. A life insurance policy is an agreement to pay a certain dollar amount upon the death of the insured individual and is meant to protect against the costs and loss of income associated with death. To earn the right of the payout an insurance company will evaluate the health, lifestyle, and age of the insured to determine a price—the premium—to be paid to the insurance company.

The product does not have to be a formal insurance policy to be considered an insurance motivation. The insurance motive is when the resource is acquired with the intent to protect loss. An individual choosing to be active religiously could be motivated by a desire to insure against hell if there is an afterlife with punishments based on our actions in this life. I know many people who participate in a lottery pool with coworkers, not because they hope to win millions, but to protect themselves if their colleagues win the lottery jackpot and quit their jobs, leaving behind everyone who chooses not to participate.

Buyer Rejection: Fear of Negative Value

In reality, not all products are worth time, money, and effort. Some products fail to deliver expectations, and when they do, they cause negative value, meaning that it harms the buyer.

Buyers are afraid of negative value, as they should be, so they are often unsure about new products that have not been proved to add value. Most buyers assume that the product does not add value unless its performance has been clearly demonstrated.

A negative value doesn't only happen with new products, so customers are always trying to maximize the value. For example, economics has a term "marginal product of labor." It refers to how much you get out of more labor, (the change in output by adding one "unit" of labor) such as hiring a new employee or an existing employee working for an additional hour. Sometimes adding more hours adds more value. Certainly, you are more productive in your second and third than the first hour, after you get into a flow. You get more value for each additional hour. However, once you reach nineteen and twenty hours of continuous work, your effectiveness declines with each additional hour. At some point, for each hour of work you produce nothing of value and eventually your productivity goes negative, and all you do is create a mess that you will have to clean up later.

Buyer Motivation: Education

Education is a universal product and the reasons for acquiring it extend across all the types of product motivations.

People who consume education love learning intrinsically; they don't expect to get something out of their education, they just enjoy the activity; they read books, listen to podcasts, watch documentaries, read blogs, and enjoy college courses.

Those who see education as an investment anticipate that what they learn and the credentials they earn will make them more valuable in the job market or otherwise make them more money. They go to college, obtain professional credentials or certificates, study online, take continuing education courses to get a return on investing their money and time.

People who pursue education as a savings vehicle expect that their knowledge will allow them to save some other resource. A single mother working two jobs may take night classes so that in the future she only needs to work one job. Her education allows her to save time to spend with her children. A plumber who started his own small business may take accounting classes to avoid the expense of paying a bookkeeper. His education allows him to save more of the money he makes through plumbing.

Many people think education, especially higher education, insures their future. They expect that earning a bachelor's degree or a master's degree protects them against low wages or unemployment.

Someone who buys education could also experience a negative value. Earning a PhD in medieval history could be an example. Someone who earns that doctorate in medieval history but doesn't secure one of the few jobs that require such credentials would find it impossible to recover the costs and time of the education. Additionally, it may make the student less employable. Many employers might not want to hire a PhD to perform a job that can be done by a high school dropout at the same hourly rates.

These buyer motivations are more than just a theoretical exercise. Your early adopters are trying to solve a problem by selecting your technology. If you can't explain it to them from their point of view, they won't use it and your technology will go unused. They don't care about the constraint breakthroughs or novel approaches. I have also seen innovators like yourself focus on one type of buyer motivation, such as savings, and ignore the other motivations. Listen first to the customers, or prospective customers, because they will tell you their motivation.

The Five Product Characteristics

In addition to understanding the motivations of the buyer, you can make adjustments to the product in order to facilitate adoption. There are five product characteristics that can accomplish that: relative advantage, improving the performance of the product; compatibility with existing processes and technologies; complexity, the time and expertise needed to implement and learn to operate the product; trialability, allowing buyers to use the product prior committing to a decision, and observability, allowing potential customers to see and assess others using the product as part of the decision process.

These characteristics are the only ways to innovate a product. In the 1962 book *Diffusion of Innovations*, Everett Rogers identified these five characteristics as either preventing or facilitating the adoption of new technology. It is important for you to make conscious product decisions because they will make it easier or more difficult for potential buyers to begin using the product.

Product Characteristic: Relative Advantage

The most common innovation for products comes from improving the performance, or usefulness, of the product, which will lead to quicker adoption and broader diffusion. Review the Grades of Innovation for how to conduct a comprehensive analysis of the relative advantage of other offerings in your industry.

Product Characteristic: Observability

I often wonder how many innovations were born with great potential only to have died without the world taking notice. Inherently observable products spread quicker and further because they allow potential users to discover the product and evaluate the performance before making a decision. Perhaps most importantly, visible products provide evidence that other people in a social group are using them. Humans love to do things that they see other people do.

Consumer wearables are inherently observable and one of the reasons that fashion trends can spread and change so quickly. In 1797, wearing a top hat resulted in the arrest of John Hetherington. John was a "haberdasher" in England. Although he did not invent the top hat he was one of the first to wear one in public. The hat's "shiny lustre… frighten timid people… several women fainted at the unusual sight, while children screamed, dogs yelped and a younger son of Cordwainer Thomas was thrown down by the crowd which collected and had his right arm broken."[29] Mr. Hetherington was arrested and arraigned before the Lord Mayor of London on January 15, 1797, on a charge of breach of the peace and inciting a riot and was required to post a £500 bond.[30] Within twenty years top hats had become popular with all social classes, even blue collar workers. Top hats would remain popular for the next one hundred years.

Product Characteristic: Trialability

Choosing to adopt innovation carries the risk of failure and negative value. Uncertainty causes people to fear the new product, which slows adoption. When potential users can use the product as part of the decision process, they will be more likely to adopt the new product. The ability to use the product prior to committing to a decision is call trialability.

AOL used trialability of the Internet to fuel its growth. AOL knew the Internet would be hard to describe to new users. It also knew that when people tried the Internet, they would want to continue to use it. In the late 1990s AOL was a fast growing provider of Internet access across the United States. In 1997 about half of all US homes with internet access had it through AOL.[31]

AOL spent over $300 million flooding the United States with promotional CDs loaded with AOL software that would enable users to begin using AOL, with a code that would allow risk-free access to the services. Jan Brandt, former chief marketing officer for AOL, said: "At one point, 50 percent of the CDs produced worldwide had an AOL logo on it." [32]

Steve Case, AOL cofounder and former CEO, explained the explosion in users and resulting valuation: "When we went public in 1992 we had less than 200,000 subscribers; a decade later the number was in the 25 million range. That helped drive our market capitalization up from $70 million at the time of the IPO to $150 billion"[33]

Product Characteristic: Compatibility

Innovations that are compatible with existing processes and technologies will be adopted quicker than those that are not compatible or that are difficult to integrate. If users cannot use the new product with existing systems, it reduces the value, sometimes to zero.

The first time I traveled internationally as a teenager I was surprised to learn that there are different electrical outlets plugs and sockets than those in the United States. It was something I had never considered because I only had used the two kinds available in North America. Worldwide there are fifteen types of outlet plugs in use. Imagine you create a new electronic device that is a 10x improvement over existing solutions. You begin manufacturing the device for worldwide distribution without making it compatible with outlets in the target markets. The innovation is compelling, but the device is immediately irrelevant because of such a simple mistake.

The incompatibility of healthcare software and systems with each other slows adoption of updated systems and capabilities to reduce costs and improve care. Healthcare could have systems that efficiently and securely exchange patient information, but as Marc Probst, a member of Health Information Technology Policy Committee, the group that made recommendations on health information infrastructure to the US federal government, said: "Presently, we lack a shared infrastructure and long-term plan to make this possible. We must adopt standards that will make it easier to share health information, so clinicians and patients have the information in the form and time they need it to make appropriate healthcare decisions,"[34] Maybe adopting interoperability standards is the only practical way forward in healthcare in the US, but coordination is not always a requirement in other industries.

Product Characteristic: Complexity

Complexity slows innovation adoption. A complex new product requires that people spend time and acquire expertise to become proficient at operating it.

Engineers and user-interface designers have made computers much easier to use over the past thirty years, which has facilitated adoption. In the early days, computer programmers wrote source code on paper and then retyped the code onto punch cards. Programmers gave the cards to an operator who would load them into a speed-reader, run the job and return the results on print-outs. This process was so complicated and cumbersome that computers were not used by anyone, except the most passionate, curious, and some say, socially challenged geeks.

Today computers are so simple to use children who lack reading or verbal skills can play games and watch videos unassisted by adults. Monitors, keyboards, the mouse, and the touchscreen took decades of development. Elena Ferrante, an author, described writing on a computer for the first time. Computers had shed their complexity and using them had become natural. Even though she describes an early computer's green screen, she captures the experience beautifully.

> *Lila began to type on the keyboard, I was speechless. It was in no way comparable to a typewriter, even an electric one. With her fingertips she caressed gray keys, and the writing appeared silently on the screen, green like newly sprouted grass... It seemed to me like the writing of God as it must have been on Sinai at the time of the Commandments, impalpable and tremendous, but with a concrete effect of purity. Magnificent, I said. I'll teach you, she said. And she taught me... our volatile discussions were imprinted on the dark well of the screen like waves without foam.*[35]

The Gang Analyzes Innovation Type 1—Products

Markus: Outsourced Development

Describe buyer motivations for your product and the five product characteristics.

Consumption:

> *My clients' intrinsic motivation would be just to have good software. Like, the software just does what it is supposed to do. A customer has a job to do, and the software helps do that job.*

Investment:

> *My clients' investment motivation is usually to create their product or enhance their existing products to generate more revenue. They spend money on development, and the result is an asset that can return more money to the company.*

Saving:

> *My clients want to save money by hiring an outsourced development shop because the costs of hiring and managing their full-time staff quickly add up and can be more than the consulting rates. It could also be that the software enables them to save money somewhere else, such as server resources or automating something that requires staff time.*

Insurance:

> *If my clients hire us, or any other outsourced development company, they may want to insure the risk of trying to manage the development internally. Years ago (when IBM was the gold standard) people used to say "Nobody ever got fired for buying IBM." So, if a project fails, but you hired a consulting firm with a good reputation, then you have someone to blame. If you do it internally and you mess up then you only have yourself to blame.*

Negative Value:

> *Many of my clients have hired outsourced development shops, spending a lot of money only to have unusable software at the end. So, there is a real risk of spending money on time and not having any usable results. I guess it could even be worse than that because it could be useful software that sucks and has lots of problems.*

Describe how you can improve your product based on the five product characteristics:

Relative Advantage:

> *The relative advantage of our services is measured by the speed and the quality of the services. I think being at industry standard is sufficient.*

Compatibility:

> *I believe that this gets to having developers that know the languages that our clients need. If we can't integrate with their tech or with what their requirements are, then we are not helpful.*

Complexity:

> *We can reduce complexity by making it easier to work with us, from contracts, to project scoping, to updates and iterations.*

Trialability:

> *Having a trialable service is difficult. I think the closest we could get is to have guaranteed or your money back. But, I have done enough design projects to know that it doesn't work in practice. I don't think I could offer a trial period.*

Observability:
> *I usually do this when we have worked on some public projects. We can show the products we have built, and that helps potential clients to see the quality of our work.*

Sarah: Interviewing Service

Describe buyer motivations for your product and the five product characteristics.

Consumption:
> *I think this is the weakest motivation. My prospects could use the service to improve their interview and communication skills because they see this area as a source of deficiency.*

Investment:
> *The strongest motivation for my service is an investment. Prospects will want to spend money on improving their interview skills when they are ready to start looking for a job so that they can get better job offers.*

Saving:
> *Prospects can be motivated to save time in their job search. The better they perform on their interviews, the quicker they can get an offer. These candidates are not worried about getting an offer; they are concerned about getting an offer as quickly as possible.*

Insurance:
> *Some potential prospects will see improving their interview skills as a way to ensure that they have all their bases covered. They might not think that it will help, but they will do it, just in case it might assist them to get an offer.*

Negative Value:
> *A prospect can be afraid that he pays and then doesn't get anything out of it. Or, maybe they pick up some interview habit that makes them worse at interviewing.*

Describe how you can improve your product based on the five product characteristics:

Relative Advantage:

> *Practicing interviewing is currently difficult. Finding someone you trust, coordinating a time and location, and then the feedback is inconsistent, and you only have one person's perspective. Picking up the phone and calling, doing an interview, getting the emailed report and paying through phone bill is a vast improvement.*

Compatibility:

> *I think the key here is to be compatible with the existing job-hunting process. Needs to feel a natural part of the job boards and recruiters. Recruiters should be recommending everyone use this service to prepare for job interviews.*

Complexity:

> *I think complexity for me means the ease to sign up for the service. I can get it close to Amazon's One-Click Checkout. Prospects just call our 1-900 number, and we charge the phone bill. The interviewer asks for the email address during the interview to send the report. I will need to make sure the report is also straightforward and easy to understand.*

Trialability:

> *I think this means that it is better to have a free trial? I can easily provide the first interview for free. I will have to plan those acquisitions costs into my financial model. I will have to provide a 1-800 number and then cover the expenses of the person conducting the interview.*

Observability:

> *This one I don't think that I can do very well. I guess the best I can do here is to have testimonials of job hunters and how the service helped them.*

Joko: Audio Algorithm

Describe buyer motivations for your product and the five product characteristics.

Consumption:

I will focus on the student market, because I know the most about it. Students can use the software to study and improve their grades and understanding of the material.

Investment:

Students will see the software as an investment because they are spending a lot of money in college and spending a little extra on this software returns much better grades.

Saving:

Students I let use the software saw that it saved them a lot of time by focusing on the most important course material.

Insurance:

There was one friend who used the software just to make sure that she wasn't missing something from the lectures or the readings.

Negative Value:

An early software version miscalculated the emphasis from a British professor and so I studied the wrong chapters and flunked an important exam.

Describe how you can improve your product based on the five product characteristics:

Relative Advantage:

There is no close substitute. What I have created is the best study guide ever invented.

Compatibility:

The software is compatible with current technology.

Complexity:

The software is very easy to use and takes a few minutes to learn.

Trialability:

I can easily let students try the software. In school, anyone who tried it was almost immediately addicted.

Observability:

It isn't the most observable software, but in a classroom during a semester every other student learned about what I was doing.

Funding

The second type of innovation involves the resources and capital needed to create, launch, and sustain innovation

One of the most efficient ways to bring great products to market is through the creation of a corporate entity, funded with venture capital equity investment and sustained with revenue and cash flow. However, those funding sources are not the only options. Taking advantage of tax income or tax benefits and donations are overlooked but often necessary funding approaches. Debt is also a funding option, but you should rarely use it as it carries significant risks.

Equity

Adam Smith is considered the father of modern economics because of the ideas he published in his 1776 book, *An Inquiry into the Nature and Causes of the Wealth of Nations*. Smith introduced the term "invisible hand," an idea that individuals pursuing their self-interest can improve society as a whole as if guided by an invisible hand. Smith wrote: "It is not from the benevolence of the butcher, the brewer, or the baker that we expect our dinner, but from their regard to their own self-interest. We address ourselves not to their humanity but to their self-love, and never talk to them of our own necessities, but of their advantages."

Society benefits from the gains of innovation, but the most powerful mechanism to help an entire society innovate is to allow individuals to benefit financially from the value creation. Ownership and the legal right to the innovation are called equity. A typical scenario is founders launch a company in which they all share the ownership. To facilitate the company's growth the founders often need to acquire more resources and cash than they own or are willing to contribute. The founders exchange a portion of ownership with investors for money or other resources invested in the company. Venture capitalists are investors who focus on making these investments in new companies. Venture capitalists raise money from other investors, and their role is to help allocate the money with the intent to generate a financial return. Equity financing is often necessary to create and commercialize innovation.

The allure of accumulated wealth motivates innovators and investors to take action and risk cash on projects that will likely fail. The wealth of Mark Zuckerberg, Jeff Bezos, Bill Gates, and the late Steve Jobs is the result of equity generated by innovation. It is standard management practice in established companies to offer managers and executives equity so that their interests are aligned with the owners', but often innovators in established companies cannot personally benefit and own the value created inside those organizations. It's hard to value the contribution of one innovator in established firms because employees benefit from the operation of the entire organization. Additionally, management and owners often see the contributions of innovators as their role as an employee.

In 1988, Warren Buffet, chairman of Berkshire Hathaway, wrote in the company's annual report: "As they say in poker, 'If you've been in the game 30 minutes and don't know who the patsy is, you're the patsy.'" When you are making equity decision, you need to protect yourself, and if you don't know who the patsy is, it is you. Accordingly, you should make decisions based on your self-interest and capture as much equity as possible and give away as little as you can. You should also expect those cofounders, team members, and investors will make decisions based on their self-interest.

Revenue

Revenue is capital obtained in return for products or services. Revenue is the mechanism to "capture the value created." You can generate revenue in several ways, but the process can be simple.

Comedian Lewis Black, known for routines that escalate to angry rants about social issues, said: "You don't want another Enron? Here's the law: If you have a company, and it can't explain in one sentence what it does, it's illegal!" While his comedy is a comment on sophisticated business practices meant to hide fraud, the best business models should be able to be explained easily. Dave McClure is a popular angel investor and startup advisor in Silicon Valley who is a big fan of simple revenue models. "I recommend you keep it simple and keep it to one or two. When you list a large number of sources, generally that tells me that you don't know how you're making money." [36]

Sustaining innovation must come from some form of revenue and every corporate entity will eventually be valued at its earnings, which is the revenue collected, less the costs to operate and deliver the revenue. Over time, if you are unable to capture the value you create, you are creating an unsustainable organization whose value will eventually be zero.

Using revenue and earnings from other products can be a source of creating and commercializing innovation. You need access to a high margin business to support it from inception to becoming revenue self-sustaining. Google is the best in the world at using the revenue from its core business to develop innovation related to its core business and in completely unrelated industries.

Tax

Government revenue and government borrowing can accelerate innovation. Government institutions have developed or funded many modern developments. The Internet was born in the early 1960s thanks to US government agencies. Engineers from the European Organization for Nuclear Research developed touchscreen displays in the early 1970s. Even Apple's release of the Siri voice-activated system spun out of a government project on artificial intelligence.

Economist Mariana Mazzucato highlights one reason that government funding is essential to long-term innovation: "Government funding is increasingly required because venture capital—which was initially thought to provide the kind of early-stage high-risk finance... is itself becoming risk-averse and short-termist, seeking returns in three to five years. Innovation, especially in science intensive areas, takes 15-20 years, not three!"[37]

Mazzucato offers global positioning systems (GPS) as an example of a valuable innovation that cost billions of dollars over twenty-seven years. GPS is a critical feature to smartphones, navigation systems, and self-driving cars.

> *The GPS was an attempt by the Department of Defense to digitize global geographic positioning to enhance the coordination and accuracy of military assets. By the mid-1990s, civilian use of GPS quickly outnumbered military utilization following the release of the technology for commercial use. Nevertheless, to this day, the US Air Force continuously develops and maintains the system, which costs $705 million annually. From 1973 to 2000, the U.S. government invested $5.6 billion in developing the system.*

Governments have the opportunity to leverage tax and make these investments on behalf of citizens to secure their future. Government investment is driven by the incentive to manage geopolitical risks of death, and loss of liberty or wealth, but like GPS, actual use of the technology can vary widely. Scientists today are building the technologies of tomorrow while innovators leverage the government investments of yesterday.

Using tax dollars to fund research is critical to innovation and so is incentivizing research and consumption of innovation by providing tax breaks. In the US, the government has provided financial incentives to help fund and consume alternative energy through various tax incentives, such as developing wind farms, manufacturing and installing solar power, and hybrid and electric vehicles.

In your approach, you should know what initiatives the government has been developing that may help you create advanced solutions. You should also explore how government financial incentives may fund portions of your efforts, either directly or indirectly through incentives to your customers.

Donations

Donations are a powerful and often under-used funding source. Donations can come in the form of money, capital, time, and talent all given without condition of something in return.

Wikipedia is the seventh most popular site in the world and is entirely supported by donations. Wikipedia receives cash donations to pay for servers and electricity and is supported by time and talent contributions of pages, edits, code, and translations. By 2008 Wikipedia represented 100 million hours of human work. Wikipedia does have 187 full-time paid staff running the organization, but that is tiny compared to the 27 million registered editors. [38]

In 2007, Oded Nov wrote a paper *What Motivates Wikipedians*, and identified eight motivations of people who contribute to the site.[39]

1. Values – Wikipedians express their personal values by helping others.
2. Social – Wikipedians use their service to engage with friends and to take part in activities viewed favorably by others.
3. Understanding – Wikipedians want to expand their knowledge and understanding.
4. Career – Wikipedians gain valuable work experience and skills that benefit them.
5. Protective – Wikipedians reduce guilt over personal privilege.
6. Enhancement – Wikipedians want to demonstrate knowledge to others.
7. Ideology – Wikipedians express support the underlying ideology of the activity (e.g. the belief that knowledge should be free).
8. Fun – Wikipedians just enjoy the activity.

Not every innovation can use donation. But, you can learn from Wikipedia to leverage the motivations of so many people who donate their time and treasure to support the site. Ask yourself if there is a way to involve others based on one of the eight Wikipedia motivations. Even if you don't pursue donations, the analysis is helpful to explore alternative interactions.

Debt

You can fund innovation through debt, but my advice is that you shouldn't. Debt is borrowing the resources needed to fund or sustain the innovation with the promise to return the resources, with interest. Debt requires you to promise a financial return, which is dangerous given the accumulative risks. Debt's appeal is that you can avoid giving up equity so that if successful, your personal equity will be worth more.

Mark Cuban sums a position on debt well, in an interview with Bloomberg. Although Cuban is explicitly talking about starting a business, the same advice applies to all types of innovation. "If you start a business and you take out a loan, you are a moron. There are so many uncertainties with starting a business, yet the one certainty you will have is paying back your loan." [40]

The Gang Analyzes Innovation Type 2—Funding

Markus: Outsourced Development

Describe how you could use each of the four funding sources.
Equity:
> *I would use equity to motivate cofounders and other valuable employees. I might have to raise some money from investors to help provide cash to grow.*

Revenue:
> *Essentially we are selling our time, or we are selling a deliverable. Revenue is easy for this business. There are a lot of customers lining up to buy already.*

Government:
> *This one's hard. I think the best I can come up with is the fact that our customers deduct our charges on their taxes. Maybe I would have to talk to a tax accountant to know what tax advantages are available to us. Like hiring military veterans for some roles.*

Donations:
> *Okay, this one's hard too. One idea might be that we could use blogs to help market our services and we might be able to get some guest spots that we could use which would assist the guest author in their career.*

Which funding source will you focus on?
> *I hope that revenue can fund almost everything. I have a good pipeline now, and margins are pretty good, so if we grow purposefully, then I might not need to be in any outside investment. Government and donations don't actually provide any other critical support.*

Sarah: Interviewing Service

Describe how you could use each of the four funding sources.

Equity:

I will use equity with cofounders, and a little for some early employees. We will likely have to raise money from investors.

Revenue:

The value is given to the interviewee, so they should pay for the service.

Government:

Maybe there are some government grants to help pay for job preparation training, such as for military veterans or former prison inmates.

Donations:

If there isn't government funding, perhaps I could pursue cash donations to help pay for the veterans. Also, I think maybe there is an opportunity for the interviewers to donate their time for several of the Wikipedia reasons. So, perhaps I could reduce my interview costs.

Which funding source will you focus on?

I had not considered donations as an important piece of my plans, but I think there is something to having interviewers be from existing companies. For example, a large tech company such as Google might provide some HR personnel time to interview specific prospects. Worst case scenario, the interviewer provides useful feedback and best case scenario, the interviewer has identified a potential candidate to bring back in for another interview with the company. This could change my model a little bit, in that I won't have to pay recruiters or other HR professionals to conduct the interview. Something I need to think about too is maybe I could charge Google to allow their staff to do the interviews. If I am using their employees, all of a sudden, I am creating value to both sides of the interview. But my main funding source will be revenue for the interview services and equity to help fund the growth.

Joko: Audio Algorithm

Describe how you could use each of the four funding sources.
Equity:

My idea will definitely require significant investment and the regular stock options.

Revenue:

The product works well and people will be willing to pay for it. Even poor students are willing to pay for it.

Government:

I am sure the government would be interested in the technology and would contract with us, once we can demonstrate that it would work for them. Or, maybe if we could get the right contacts, they might be willing to help us develop government capabilities.

Donations:

Maybe I could "crowd-source" some recorded audio to improve my dataset.

Which funding source will you focus on?

Most likely equity and revenue will be important in the beginning and government might become more important as the software gets more sophisticated. I am conflicted about using government money because it can keep people safe but it can also be used to spy on an innocent population.

Information

> *Information wants to be free. Information also wants to be expensive. ...That tension will not go away.*
> — Stewart Brand

The third type of innovation is about your choice to accumulate or disseminate information. Keeping information a secret brings power to the holder, but sharing information also brings power to the giver.

The natural state of information is unorganized and brief. The time the sun rises, for example, can be observed each day. But data about the sunrise is not naturally organized. If the time is not captured, then the information is quickly forgotten. Computers have allowed us to create, capture, and hold information at an unprecedented rate. But still more information remains uncollected, even though it is valuable.

You grow power from information because capturing it is inherently asymmetric. Asymmetric information means that one side of an interaction has more knowledge than the other side, giving it an advantage, which can make the outcome obvious to the party with the information.

Information asymmetry is like being the only player at the poker table who knows what cards all the other players are holding. If you know all the cards, the outcome is obvious to you, but still a surprise to all the other players. Most players prefer situations where information is symmetrical, meaning all sides have identical information. At the beginning of your poker game, the information about what each player holds exists briefly, in the mind of each player (like a silo). Information's natural state is like this, unorganized and brief. But, let's assume that somehow you can capture what other players hold and organize the information in a way to modify the way you choose to play. Now your chances of winning are assured. Over time you will even understand how any particular player prefers to play hands given similar circumstances. Over time you will know more about their tendencies than they know about themselves. If the other players are not aware you have this information, you will appear to be a fantastic poker player.

You can do two things with the information you capture; either accumulate it for your advantage or disseminate it.

Accumulate

You can capture or access information and leverage it to create value for your product, your customers, or yourself. If you have valuable information that nobody else has it means they depend on you for access to the information.

Many prominent companies accumulate information. Since its foundation, Netflix has collected information regarding the viewing habits and preferences of its subscribers. Netflix leverages its information to make content purchasing decisions and to create its proprietary content, custom tailored to the company's customers. Facebook has accumulated social connections of users across the world, including personal preferences, which the company leverages to provide advertisers with relevant audiences.

Disseminate

Alternatively, you can capture or access information and leverage the dissemination of the information to create value for your product, your customers, or yourself.

Some prominent information activists, such as Richard Stallman, want all information to be available. "I believe that all generally useful information should be free. By 'free' I am not referring to price, but rather to the freedom to copy the information and to adapt it to one's own uses… When information is generally useful, redistributing it makes humanity wealthier no matter who is distributing and no matter who is receiving."

At times dissemination is in the public interest. WikiLeaks, for example, acquires secret and classified information from anonymous sources involving war, spying, and corruption. WikiLeaks' goal is "to bring important news and information to the public. One of [its] most important activities is to publish original source material alongside [its] news stories so readers and historians alike can see evidence of the truth."

Other examples of information dissemination include Kelly Blue Book, which provides vehicle valuation information to consumers, and Zillow, which provides home real estate appraisal services. Historically, buyers in these two industries did not have access to these estimates.

The Gang Analyzes Innovation Type 3—Information

Describe how you could use information dissemination and information accumulation with your product.

Markus: Outsourced Development

> *This is difficult. I don't think there is any information that we can release back to nature or put in a zoo.*

Sarah: Interviewing Service

> *This has made me think that perhaps there is an additional business line in the future. If we can accumulate a lot of information about a candidate's background, ability to improve in a job interview, but also include our technical assessment of their skills, such as a software coding assessment, we could begin to advise medium-sized companies on their hiring practices.*
>
> *For example, a medium-sized company might know what they want in a candidate, but they might not be as good at assessing and selecting candidates. Their selection process might be flawed, due to their internal interview process and how they rank candidates due to the results of their interview process. We could use our information to help them identify the ideal candidate.*
>
> *The information we can capture and integrate could also be made free to our customers. They will want to know how they compare to other similar interviewees and how they progress about their peers. We can share all this information with them.*

Joko: Audio Algorithm

My algorithm is powerful, and I process a lot of data. I think we are accumulating the information because it is very valuable to our insights. As time goes on, the algorithm improves as there are more ways an individual can verbally communicate what they think about what they are saying. Additionally, the more accents and languages we include then the better the results will be over time.

I don't think we could disseminate our information, but we could disseminate the analysis of the data. For example, we can take public data, such as everything a politician says publicly, analyze it and then share the results with the world. I am not sure that we will ever be able to say if a politician is lying, but we could provide other context like whether what they are saying is important to them or not. If a politician says that he really wants a healthcare bill to be voted on and passed by Congress, we could tell you whether he felt confident about that or not.

Brand

Branding makes adopting innovation easier because branding is more than just a name and a logo. In English, the word brand comes from the German "der Brand," which means fire. The meaning comes from the practice of burning a symbol onto the hide of cattle to help ranchers identify their animals.

The concept lives on, in that a brand is a way to identify one product quickly, or in other words, the brand is an impression burned into the mind of the customer that summarizes the value of the product. An Apple logo impresses differently than a Dell logo. The Tesla customer identifies with the Tesla product very differently than the Ferrari customer relates to the Ferrari. The brand personality of the New York investment bank Goldman Sachs is hard-working, ruthless, analytical, and closed. Goldman Sachs is the opposite from the clown mascot for McDonald's. Ronald McDonald's personality is open, friendly, creative, and outgoing.

Elon Musk described the connection between brand and product: "Brand is just a perception, and perception will match reality over time. Sometimes it will be ahead, other times it will be behind. But a brand is simply a collective impression some have about a product."

Over time, however, your brand perception will either be ahead, behind or match your product. But, with an innovative product, time can be a killer. When your brand perception lags behind the product, the perception will slow or stop product adoption. Innovative product adoption is inherently difficult when brand perception lags the product so if you can mend the brand image you will increase adoption. If your product can manage to survive, over time opinion will merge with product performance, despite branding deficiencies.

Positive brand perception that is ahead of the product will facilitate adoption in the beginning. But, if you don't improve your product, the forward perception will not be sustainable, and your customers will become disillusioned because the impression doesn't meet their expectations.

Creating Your Brand

Every element of the brand contributes to the overall impression, and the impression is always about the form customers expect, and what customers expect is expressed in the industry standard. These details are well understood and can be well crafted by professional management.

What you need to do is first orientate yourself to your industry standard. In most cases, matching the brand to the industry standard is sufficient. If you want your brand to be a source of innovation, then your branding decisions will be in contrast to the industry standard.

Let me put this another way. Most likely you just want your brand to not harm you. To do that, just accept the industry standard. Give the people what they want.

If you want a brand to distinguish you, then you need to craft your brand specifically in contrast to the industry standard.

Levers of Perception

You have three levers to innovate with your brand to communicate effectively with customers about your product. Jean-Noël Kapferer outlined these levers in *The New Strategic Brand Management*: Physique, Customer Identity, and Personality.[41]

Physique of the Brand

Brand physique is all the physical elements associated with the product. These physical components include the product design itself, the product functionality, brand name, the brand name phonetics, brand logo, brand colors, website design, word selection, location, language, and the race, gender, physique, and nationality of the people involved.

Customer Identity

Customer identity is how your customers want to be perceived by themselves and others. Your brand either reinforces or destroys their identity desires. If your brand represents creativity and your customers want to appear predictable and reliable, then your brand communicates the opposite of what your customer wants.

People often confuse identity with "target customers." For example, an accounting software program may focus on chief financial officers of companies between $15M and $200M in revenue. These CFO targets may want to be perceived by others in the company as cautious and therefore only consider industry standard options. Alternatively, the CFO targets may want others to see them as creative and open to considering more experimental and risky options.

We use brands to influence how others see us but also how we view ourselves, which isn't always the same thing. You may choose to own a Lamborghini supercar so that others will see you as youthful, aggressive, and wealthy. But owning a Lamborghini carries a special meaning to you personally, because to you the car means that you are confident that you escaped the poverty of your youth. Owning an exotic Italian supercar means that you finally don't have to be anxious about walking to school in the snow with a hole in your shoes and going to bed hungry again.

Brand Personality

Your brand is a personality of your organization that needs to be in sync with the customer expectation of brand identity. A shortcut way to create a brand personality is to use a spokesperson or character to lend an established personality to a product. Many modern psychologists believe that there are five basic dimensions of personality, they call the "Big 5" personality traits: extraversion, agreeableness, conscientiousness, neuroticism, and openness.[42][43][44]

PERSONALITY	HIGH	LOW
Extraversion	Outgoing, Talkative, Active	Reserved, Loner, Quiet
Agreeableness	Friendly, Trusting, Lenient	Analytical, Ruthless, Critical
Conscientiousness	Efficient, Hard-working, Well-organized	Easy-Going, Negligent, Lazy, Disorganized

PERSONALITY	HIGH	LOW
Neuroticism	Nervous, Emotional, Worried	Confident, Unemotional, Calm
Openness	Curious, Creative, Imaginative	Cautious, Conventional, Down-to-earth

Any brand personality you create will have elements of the five personalities. These traits will be high, low, or balanced. For example, your brand will have some level of extraversion, fitting somewhere in the high-to-low spectrum of the trait.

Extraversion

High extraversion personalities love a party and love being around other people. High extraversion is excitability, sociability, talkativeness, assertiveness, and high amounts of emotional expressiveness. Individuals who are high in extraversion are outgoing and tend to gain energy in social situations.

Low extraversion personalities are introverts; they are more reserved. Introverts tend to be quiet, low-key, deliberate, and disengaged from the social world. Introversion does not mean shy or depressed. The introvert just prefers to be alone and needs less social stimulation.

Agreeableness

High agreeableness personalities desire cooperation and social harmony. Agreeable individuals value getting along with others. This personality dimension includes attributes such as friendliness, trust, altruism, kindness, affection and other prosocial behaviors.

Low agreeableness personalities are analytical, ruthless in their pursuit, and critical of others. Low agreeableness is useful in situations that require tough or absolute objective decisions, such as critics and scientists.

Conscientiousness

High conscientiousness personalities have good impulse control and goal-directed behaviors, are efficient, organized, and mindful of details. Conscientious personalities avoid trouble and achieve high levels of success through purposeful planning and persistence. Conscientious individuals can be compulsive perfectionists and workaholics.

Unconscientious personalities are easy-going and can appear negligent, lazy, and disorganized. They will experience many fleeting pleasures but may be unreliable, lack ambition, and fail to stay within the lines.

Neuroticism

Neuroticism is a personality trait of moodiness and emotional instability. Individuals high in this trait tend to experience mood swings, nervousness, irritability, and sadness. People low in this trait will tend to be more confident, stable, and emotionally resilient. Everyone shows some signs of neurosis, but we differ in our degree of suffering and our specific symptoms of distress.

Openness

Openness is a personality trait of imagination and insight. People who are high in this trait have a broad range of interests, tend to be more curious and creative in any discipline, such as mathematics, logic, artistic and metaphorical use of language, music composition or performance.

Personalities low in openness are often much more cautious and may struggle with abstract thinking. They prefer the plain, straightforward, and obvious. Closed people prefer familiarity, and they are resistant to change.

The Gang Analyzes Innovation Type 4—Brand

Markus: Outsourced development

What impression do you want to convey with your brand?

I want to convey creativity and innovation, but with predictable results. That is a tricky combination, but clients want something original but reliable. I want them to have the impression that we can deliver on their projects.

Describe how customers in your industry want your brand to make others perceive them.

> Customers want to look smart and talented. Clients are working on important company projects that will impact their careers. So, they want to look like they got the best that the company can buy. It doesn't have to be the most expensive or the highest quality.

Describe what your brand makes customers feel about themselves.

> Customers want to build confidence in themselves about their management decisions.

Highlight your brand personalities.

> I know this might be weird, but I see two personalities. One for design and another for software development. The left brain is analytical, and the right brain is creative. Our brand has to balance both sides of the brain

For the creative brain:

Personality	High	Low
Conscientiousness	Efficient, Hard-working, Well-organized	**Easy-Going, Negligent, Lazy, Disorganized**
Agreeableness	**Friendly, Trusting, Lenient**	Analytical, Ruthless, Critical
Neuroticism	Nervous, Emotional, Worried	Confident, Unemotional, Calm
Openness	**Curious, Creative, Imaginative**	Cautious, Conventional, Down-to-earth
Extraversion	**Outgoing, Talkative, Active**	Reserved, Loner, Quiet

For the analytical brain:

Personality	High	Low
Conscientiousness	**Efficient, Hard-working, Well-organized**	Easy-Going, Negligent, Lazy, Disorganized
Agreeableness	Friendly, Trusting, Lenient	**Analytical, Ruthless, Critical**
Neuroticism	Nervous, Emotional, Worried	**Confident, Unemotional, Calm**
Openness	Curious, Creative, Imaginative	**Cautious, Conventional, Down-to-earth**
Extraversion	Outgoing, Talkative, Active	**Reserved, Loner, Quiet**

Sarah: Interviewing Service

What impression do you want to convey with your brand?

The impression I want people to have with my brand is that they have a partner in the job search. I want my customers to feel like this isn't just a transaction, but that we care about them and like we are part of their team while they are searching. I want them not to feel alone.

Describe how customers in your industry want your brand to make others perceive them.

People want to appear prepared and professional. I want people to be proud that people know they use my service and not embarrassed. If my customers don't want people to know that they used us, then that is not good for us.

Describe what your brand makes customers feel about themselves.

People want to confirm to themselves that they have personal value during this process.

Highlight your brand personalities.

Personality	High	Low
Conscientiousness	**Efficient, Hard-working, Well-organized**	Easy-Going, Negligent, Lazy, Disorganized
Agreeableness	**Friendly, Trusting, Lenient**	Analytical, Ruthless, Critical
Neuroticism	Nervous, Emotional, Worried	**Confident, Unemotional, Calm**
Openness	Curious, Creative, Imaginative	**Cautious, Conventional, Down-to-earth**
Extraversion	**Outgoing, Talkative, Active**	Reserved, Loner, Quiet

Joko: Audio Algorithm

What impression do you want to convey with your brand?

I want people to be in awe of technology. I know that feeling will change over time as it becomes more commonplace, but I want people to embrace advanced technology and not be afraid. I want them to feel like it is magical.

Describe how customers in your industry want your brand to make others perceive them.

Students want to be perceived as smart and hard-working and they want the software to reinforce the perception.

Describe what your brand makes customers feel about themselves.

Students want to feel prepared.

Highlight your brand personalities.

Personality	High	Low
Conscientiousness	**Efficient, Hard-working, Well-organized**	Easy-Going, Negligent, Lazy, Disorganized
Agreeableness	Friendly, Trusting, Lenient	**Analytical, Ruthless, Critical**
Neuroticism	Nervous, Emotional, Worried	**Confident, Unemotional, Calm**
Openness	**Curious, Creative, Imaginative**	Cautious, Conventional, Down-to-earth
Extraversion	Outgoing, Talkative, Active	**Reserved, Loner, Quiet**

Channel

> *These are the new leads. These are the Glengarry leads. And to you they're gold, and you don't get them. Why? Because to give them to you would be throwing them away. They're for closers.*
> —Glengarry Glen Ross

The fifth type of innovation is your channel—the way you reach customers. Your channel includes both marketing and sales; your marketing channel is the way to communicate information with your potential clients, and the sales channel is the way to distribute the product physically.

Marketing and sales are simply a process of persuasion, designed to get the message and content right to capture the interest of the target, create desire, and lead to the action you want. As a result, most people focus on trying to get the right message to their targets, which is, of course, necessary, but your innovation strategy should concentrate on the way you share the message. Communication theorist Marshall McLuhan famously claimed: "The *medium* is the message" and so the channel you use is more important than the message itself. The channel you choose is the most important message because it influences how the message itself is perceived.

Sales (Distribution of Products and Services)

Channels can feel theoretical and confusing, so let me give you a real-world example. In small business accounting, Intuit's QuickBooks holds a near monopoly. More than 3.7 million small businesses in the United States use QuickBooks and QuickBooks' share of retail units in the business accounting category reached 94.2 percent in 2008.[45]

Xero is a New Zealand-based software company designed to break the QuickBooks monopoly by creating an updated, cloud-based software. In June 2014, Xero topped the Forbes magazine "100 most innovative growth companies" list.[46] To have a chance to compete against QuickBooks, Xero needs to use each channel type to communicate different messages.

Xero Influencers

Xero builds software that makes it easier for a business accountant to manage several clients. Xero builds a relationship with the accountants so that they are likely to recommend using Xero software. Accountants are in the business of accounting, not selling software, so the purpose of the accountant's recommendation is incidental and not central to his work. But, the recommendation of an influencer is extremely persuasive to potential customers. Xero's message by using this medium is that accountants will recommend the best accounting software. Without this channel, Xero loses credibility as a viable alternative to QuickBooks.[47]

Xero Alliances

Xero designed its software to be able to integrate other software applications into the accounting functions. Creating an app marketplace can help in several ways. Not every user needs all specialized features, so instead of building those features in the software, Xero built the basic accounting features and then allows other app developers to build things to integrate with the Xero feature set. This approach improves the Xero solution because the alliances with the software developers allow Xero to have niche solutions for their customers. The alliances also eliminate some barriers to adoption because customers can bring their existing technology and integrate quickly to a new accounting software. Xero's message through this medium is you do not have to accept limitations to your accounting software. Without this channel, Xero tells potential customers that they will have to make concessions and they should carefully consider the pros and cons.

Xero Partnerships

Xero is a startup in an industry with an existing ecosystem of software and consultants. Instead of fighting the industry standards, Xero leverages the ecosystem, including consultants who make money by selling software and earning a referral fee and by charging for implementing and servicing their recommendations. Xero maintains a partnership program with these consultants to compensate them for sales of Xero software. The program also refers service business back to the consultants, even when Xero acquires the customer through another channel. Xero's message through this medium is that the client is never alone, but that there are always experts ready to help. Without this medium, Xero communicates to prospective customers that they should be willing and able to implement and support the accounting software by themselves.

Xero Direct Sales

Customers can access Xero's website directly and sign up for the software. Potential customers can review material on the website and immediately start a chat with an online representative or ask a Xero employee to contact them to answer questions and finalize the sales process. If needed, Xero employees can also help potential customers navigate the app marketplace and make a referral to accountants or software consultants. Xero's message with this medium is that Xero's customer service is world class. Without the medium, Xero communicates that the software is expensive to implement and use and difficult to learn.

Xero Direct Delivery

Xero's only method of software delivery is through the web. Additionally, potential customers can sign up for free trials to test the software before purchase. Xero's message with this medium is modern accounting software should not be installed on a computer in your office, and you will not regret signing up for Xero. Without this medium, Xero would communicate that the software is behind industry standards and customers should be cautious during the sales cycle because customers can get locked into using the software.

Selecting Your Channels

The purpose of the channel is to cultivate a positive association, reduce uncertainty, and motivate action. Crafting your channel strategy starts with organizing all you understand about the industry standards and what those channels communicate. Any mediums you use or don't use will communicate something, either positive or negative. This signal you send out in the industry through your channels is your source of innovation.

Direct: Sales and Delivery

A direct sales channel is when the producer and the final consumer deal directly with each other. The method of interaction can occur face-to-face, over the phone, on the web, or by email order. You must have a direct sales channel if your product requires expertise to close the deal or if you introduce a new technology or process to the industry.[48]

Indirect: Sales

An indirect sales model is when at least one intermediary stands between the producer and the final consumer. There are three kinds of indirect models: partnerships, alliances, and influencers. Your goals for indirect sales must not be to avoid selling. Your goals for indirect sales are to reach new or specific markets that you cannot economically or structurally reach yourself and to offer services associated with your product that you cannot provide yourself.

You can use indirect channels only when you have a well-documented sales process, you face existing global demand that a partner can fulfill, and it is important to grow quickly to gain or protect market share.[49] An indirect sales channel is not available to high-grade innovations. Grades B, C, or D do not normally have an established sales process, and global demand may not exist.

Many innovators are attracted to indirect sales because they want to focus on the creative aspects of innovation and avoid persuading customers. However, nearly every new product must first be sold by its creator. Channel partners will rarely suggest new and unproven solutions to their clients. At some point, lasting products are accepted by the market, and then you can access an indirect channel. Incorporating an indirect channel to your strategy will create conflict because you will still sell direct and may find yourself competing against your indirect partners.

Indirect: Partnership

Indirect partnerships rely on firms that identify, sell, and service solutions. For Xero, this indirect channel consists of consultants who earn service fees for implementing and supporting the software. Partnerships are standard for software produced for corporate clients because the software is often complicated, requires customization, and customers need ongoing support after the sale. Like Xero, the software company engages with an indirect channel consulting firm to resell the software. The consulting company makes money directly from the software company for selling the software and from the customer for consulting services.

An indirect partner does not create a solution but represents the producers to the final consumer. The channel's business goals are to find the best products for its customers, grow its own business with new solutions and services, and provide services that the channel provides better than the producers.

Indirect: Alliance

An indirect alliance differs from an indirect partnership because an alliance produces something itself and does not represent any other producers. Alliances are like Xero's app integrations. MailChimp is an email marketing service that uses an alliance with Xero. In Xero's App Marketplace, MailChimp delivers a plug-in that allows the final consumer to integrate Xero and MailChimp services.

An alliance makes money by selling and servicing its product but uses mutually beneficial opportunities to collaborate with other producers without being entirely dependent on another firm. The goals of alliances are to enhance a product and leverage other producers' marketing power or customers.

Indirect: Influencer

Influencers are in the business of providing advice based on their expertise and are extremely effective in their recommendations. Influencers are Xero's accountants who recommend accounting software but are not in the business of selling software. Influencers are not always compensated for their recommendations.

The Gang Analyzes Innovation Type 5-Channel

Markus: Outsourced development

What are your industry's standard direct and indirect channels?

The standard is each group hires a sales development team and marketing department to market and sell its services.

What is your direct channel approach?

Our approach is what we have been currently doing, manage sales directly.

Is the sales process documented and can it easily be communicated to sales people?

No. The sales process is very consultative, and clients like to talk to the person that will manage the project (the person who knows what they are talking about). Of course, a salesperson is needed to start the conversation and to close the sale. I hate that whole process, but I love sitting down with clients and learning how I can help them.

Is there an existing demand that partners can fulfill based on their skills and availability to customers?

No.

What do you want to communicate with your channel?

I want to express that the entire organization services you and that we are available to help support you from the beginning to the end.

Sarah: Interviewing Service

What are your industry's standard direct and indirect channels?

I think to look at it this way, recruiters are the indirect channels, and the direct channels are individuals working their personal network to get introductions to job opportunities.

What is your direct channel approach?

> *Our direct approach will be through the advertising on the web for prospects to call us and try out the service. Eventually, if we expand to offer recruiting services, we will compete with indirect channels.*

Is the sales process documented and can it easily be communicated to sales people?

> *Yes, I can do this easily. I know how to create a sales system.*

Is there an existing demand that partners can fulfill based on their skills and availability to customers?

> *I have a lot of sales experience, and recruiters get paid on commissions. They want a product that is ready. If they send a candidate that isn't ready, not only do they miss out on commission but they also risk damaging their reputation with their client.*

Describe potential indirect channel, alliance, and influencer relationships.

> *I want recruiters to see us as a free service (to them) to help their candidates be better prepared. From a recruiter standpoint, they get a better-prepared candidate, which means higher close rates and faster commissions.*

What do you want to communicate with your channel?

> *I want to communicate that people who are serious about their job search use the interview preparation to get ready.*

Joko: Audio Algorithm

What are your industry's standard direct and indirect channels?

> *There are software companies that can benefit from indirect channels, especially those companies that sell to other businesses. But I think all of my distribution will come through a website and most marketing will be by word of mouth and the media talking about the technology.*

Is the sales process documented and can it easily be communicated to sales people?

> *No.*

Is there an existing demand that partners can fulfill based on their skills and availability to customers?

No.

What do you want to communicate with your channel?

I want to communicate that the technology is so good that users will come to us.

Network

> *Facebook is quite entrenched and has a network effect. It's hard to break into a network once it's formed.*
> —Elon Musk

The sixth type of innovation is a network. A network is just a group of interconnected things. You use many kinds of networks every day. Some are digital, such as the Internet, cell phones, and Wi-Fi. Some are social, such as your connections on Facebook, your coworkers, your family, and your friends. Some are physical, such as highways, airports, cities, and countries.

The value of connecting to a network depends on the number of other things already connected to the network. Alumni networks at top universities can be more valuable than the education itself, because of the influential and accomplished people who are already attached to the school network. Even as higher education is democratized, education from important institutions remains valuable because of those networks.

There are four basic building blocks of a network. First is a node, which is an individual or a thing that can be connected to other nodes. Second is a connector, which is a node with a large number of connections. The third is a connection, the way in which two or more nodes interact. The relationship can be strong or weak. And fourth is an interchange, which is something to be exchanged between nodes.

Metcalfe's Law states that the value of a telecommunications network is proportional to the square of the number of connected users of the system. What this means is that as more things are added to the network, each part of the network becomes more valuable. For example, if the value of a network to a single user is one dollar for each other user in the network, then a network of size 10 has a total value of roughly one hundred dollars. When the network increases by ten times, the value of the network increases by one hundred times. When the network grows from ten to one hundred users the network has a total value of roughly

$10,000. Metcalfe's Law and the value of the networks is a compelling reason why many innovators turn to the power of networks to enhance the value of their products.

It's hard to imagine a telephone separated from a network, but if the technology could exist without the network, the value would be reduced to almost zero. The more people who own telephones connected to other phones, the more valuable the phone is to each owner. Some numbers are connectors, such as those owned by the IRS or utility companies, because they have a relationship with a high number of other individuals and receive more calls than other telephones.

Two telephone nodes can make only one connection, but five nodes can make ten connections, and fourteen nodes can make ninety-one connections.

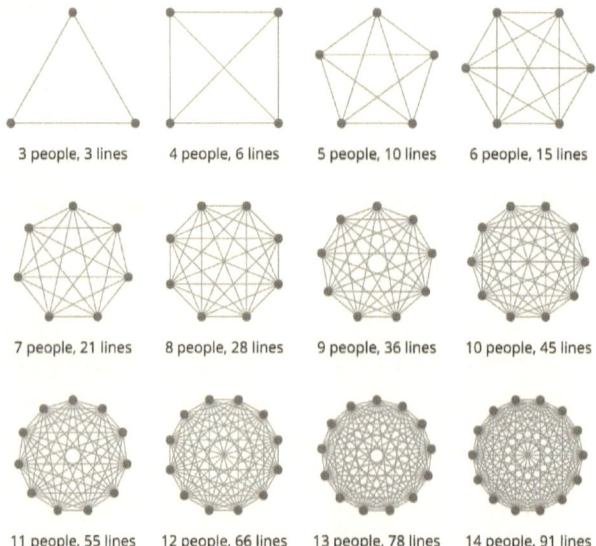

This positive growing value is often called "network effect." Over time, this effect can create a "bandwagon effect" as more people join in a positive feedback loop. However, the network can experience adverse effects, where more users make a product less valuable, such as traffic or network "congestion."

Facebook provides the ability to connect groups of friends, and the network becomes more valuable to each user as more users across the globe are connected. On Facebook, each user who creates an account is a node. The connection is being "friends" with others. These can be strong links, such as close friends you see daily, or a weak link such as a high school classmate you have not seen for several years. A connector is someone very social with a lot of friends. Individuals interchange messages, posts, likes, and other interactions that occur on the website.

Southwest Airlines uses a network of airports to operate its business. Each destination is a node. Southwest has used smaller airports in the major urban markets. Southwest has historically avoided connectors, or the major, most-congested airports because that meant more competition with other airlines and longer turnaround times. The connection is a geographical location of the airport. Some cities have a larger population, so the relationship is enduring. Other cities have a smaller population, so the connection is weak. The network interchange is each plane's passengers.

Amazon uses a distribution network to fulfill its orders. Each customer's shipping address is a node. Its fulfillment centers are connectors since each center connects to many customers. The relationship is the purchasing history with Amazon, and these relationships can be powerful if the customer makes several purchases, or limited if the customer only makes occasional purchases. The interchange is cash and product.

Network Strategies

You can use two different sets of innovation strategies to deploy a network. These strategies were defined in a book by Carl Shapiro and Hal Varian *Information Rules: A Strategic Guide to the Network Economy*. The plans are open/closed and compatible/incompatible.[50]

A closed network is when a firm keeps control of the innovation as a proprietary technology. An open network means the technology is available to various individuals or firms to build products complying with the standard, either for free by making it available via license.

Whether you can choose an open or closed strategy is based on your influence in the industry. Startups and firms trying to break into an existing customer base benefit from open network strategies. As the industry shifts, strategies for the open networks are likely to change as well. Firms with a presence and an existing customer base typically want closed systems to maintain control. Closed networks lock in customers to a technology and allow the creator to direct control over the technology and the industry.

A compatible network means that changes in the technology are designed to be used with the existing systems. An incompatible network means that changes in the technology require the adoption of an entirely new network. Compatible or incompatible network strategies are based on the grade of the innovation.

There are four strategy combinations, closed/compatible, closed/incompatible, open/incompatible, and open/compatible.

Closed Standard and Compatible to Existing Network

When a firm controls the technology and issues an update that is compatible with existing services, customers are offered an improved solution. This strategy typically works well for AA and A grades and firms with industry influence.

Microsoft's launch of Xbox One is an example of starting a compatible product on a closed network. Microsoft offers subscriptions to Microsoft Live, a service for the gaming console Xbox. This network allows 48 million gamers to play against other people across the Internet.[51] Xbox Live is a closed network because each player must use a Microsoft Xbox to connect to the network. When Microsoft launched its new Xbox One console, gamers using Xbox One could connect to Xbox Live, play Xbox 360 games and play with or against players using Xbox 360.

Closed Standard and Incompatible to Existing Network

A closed and incompatible strategy is the boldest and riskiest of the four network approaches. This option is only available to startups and smaller organizations with speculative innovation grading of B, C, or D. Entrants do not have the same problems as incumbents such as backward compatibility or legacy commitments that cannibalize sales of existing products and alienate loyal customers.

Most messaging and chat applications are closed and incompatible. Blackberry developed proprietary BlackBerry Messenger, which until 2013 was only available on BlackBerry phones. Blackberry Messenger is not compatible with other messenger apps, such as WhatsApp, Facebook Messenger, Skype Instant Messenger, and QQ. Every one of these messaging apps is closed because each is maintained by a different company, and they are all incompatible because each new app technology does not work with other apps' networks.

Open Standard and Incompatible to Existing Network

An open and incompatible strategy occurs when there is no continuation in the existing network, with a change to a speculative grade of B, C, or D. The change in technology becomes the new open standard that can be supplied by many vendors.

Listening to music in automobiles is an example of open and incompatible changes. In the 1970s compact cassettes became a popular method of listening to music in cars. The cassette technology was open, and many vendors patented variations in the technology, launched, and sold versions of cassettes. The compact disc (CD), which was co-developed by Philips and Sony, launched a migration of the technology used in automobiles. The CD was an open technology but incompatible with the cassette technology. Incompatibility meant consumers needed to replace cassette players with after-market CD players or other adapters to listen to CDs in the car. In the 2000s consumers traded CDs for MP3 players, such as the iPod. Again, the MP3 technology was open, but MP3s were not compatible and required new approaches to integration.

Open Standard and Compatible to Existing Network

Open and compatible is where there is an agreed upon, open standard for the network and this standard can be supplied by many vendors. This combination is typically AA and A grades and is very friendly to consumers. This is a strategy for a firm that can pair networks with industry-leading core processes or economies of scale.

Launching a new fax machine is an example of an open and compatible network. A fax machine uses telephone lines to transfer documents. The phone line is an open network, and new machines are compatible with the network and can send faxes to other machines connected to the network.

The Gang Analyzes Innovation Type 6—Network

Markus: Outsourced Development

This isn't applicable to me.

Sarah: Interviewing Service

I don't think that I have a network opportunity. There are some aspects of a network, but I don't think the value to any user of my customers improves with more users. Maybe if I changed my idea, but I want to help the job-seekers, not recruiters or companies directly.

Joko: Audio Algorithm

Describe a closed standard/compatible network for your idea.

I think this type of network is what I had envisioned. I want to control the technology but make it available and compatible with current hardware and software.

Describe a closed standard/incompatible network for your idea.

If I were to make it incompatible with existing networks I think it would mean that I would develop my own hardware. The downside of this is students would have to buy new hardware and I would have to design and manufacture the hardware. I had to think for a long time about the benefits of building incompatibility. When we talked about the product one of the weaknesses was that the solution was not really observable. But, if students had to come to class and put a device on their desk to record the lecture, it would make it much more visible. I don't know if the trade-off is worth it because of all the problems we might have getting into hardware. Maybe it would make the software look cooler if it needed its own hardware, but if anyone opened up the box they would see a fairly basic recording device.

Describe an open standard/compatible network for your idea.

Making the software open could be interesting. Perhaps I could open up the algorithm as a platform for other developers to incorporate. I don't want to do this because it means I could lose control over the technology.

Describe an open standard/incompatible network for your idea.

This type of network doesn't really make sense for my idea. I would make it open and incompatible with existing technology? Seems that would make it much more difficult to adopt. I am not iterating on an existing capability.

Core Process

> *Design is not just what it looks like and feels like. Design is how it works.*
> —Steve Jobs

Each organization maintains two main types of processes: the core process, which is the means by which the organization creates value, and the enabling process, which sustains the organization and enables the organization to perform its basic function.

The seventh type of innovation is the core process, which is manufacturing for a manufacturer, software development for a software company, cooking for restaurants, and surgery for surgeons.

Innovation in the core process is created by reducing the use of time, materials, labor, and other resources, cutting unnecessary processes, and reducing the variability of the outputs. There are many methodologies and tools organization use, such as Six Sigma, that have a history of creating innovations out of processes.

Teams turn to these commonly accepted tools to improve repeatable tasks and still fail because they execute the methodology without understanding the overall strategy or how to use the tool effectively. As a result, the methods are blamed as ineffective, the results dramatically underperform, or worse, the team engages in innovation theater.

The core process is either standardizable work or original work. Standardizable work is completed from core processes where the outputs are identical or very similar to each other. Manufacturing is a perfect example of standardizable work because it requires near identical inputs, produces near identical outputs, and the process for each product is identical to every other unit. Examples of standardizable manufacturing work include Toyota automobiles, McDonald's hamburgers, Nike shoes, and Apple computers.

Original work is completed from core processes where each result is unique. Examples of original work include designing Toyota automobiles, inventing the newest McDonald's hamburger, creating Lebron's next Nike shoe, and developing Apple's latest computer. Each original work, such as design and software development, shares some essential characteristics, but each work requires iteration and judgment.

Standardizable Work

Manufacturing has benefited immensely from improvements to standardizing work, such as adopting the assembly line during the industrial revolution. Before the invention of the assembly line craftsmen would create each part of the product and then assemble the final product. The assembly line changed that process by standardizing each of the parts, which reduced the variability in the final product and only required workers to specialize in one part of the assembly. The assembly line moves the product around the workers, instead of the workers around the product. These improvements reduced time and process, and required fewer workers. Standardizing work is fantastic because improving and refining the process is complex, dynamic, and complicated. Therefore, standardizable work is infinitely improvable.

There should not be variability in the end product of standardizable work. The definition of quality in repeatable work is very low variability. Quality is not defined in qualitative terms, such as product performance. Each Big Mac should be like all the other Big Macs, and the way to do that is to assemble all Big Macs in the defined process that results in the perfect Big Mac. You may have a preference on what makes a good hamburger, but a quality Big Mac is one that meets the criteria of a Big Mac. Each Toyota Corolla should be like all the other Corollas. Each Nike shoe, like all the others. And each MacBook should be indistinguishable from any other MacBook.

Manufacturers and others have pursued quality improvement for decades. They have used various methodologies that are designed to lead innovators to reduce the differences between each product. Total Quality Management, Quality Circles, and Business Process Reengineering are some of these methodologies.

Six Sigma

Six Sigma is focused on measuring and improving the variability in products by statistical terms. Six Sigma answers this question: How many of the products meet the definition of a quality product? Six Sigma provides a framework to improve the answer. Six Sigma's name refers to its goal to reduce defects to three standard deviations, or 3.4 per million opportunities, or 99.99966 percent accuracy. The Six Sigma process uses the five-step DMAIC process.

Define the goals. Measure current status. Analyze the process and systems to understand cause and effect. Improve the process. Control and monitor the process to continue to eliminate defects.

DMAIC is helpful for any repeatable process. Know what the ideal product should be, know where you currently are, understand what causes problems, fix the causes, and then measure to make sure that the problems were fixed and stay fixed. How many times have you been a part of a decision-making process that skipped one or four of these steps? The most typical mistake is to proceed to step four and leave out step five because the team or the leader has an intuition on steps one, two, and three and is so confident the process is improved that there is no reason to proceed to step five.

Reducing the variability in repeatable processes can be quantified and measured because the ideal result is consistent. There is no moving target defining what quality should be. If there is a moving target then you do not have a repeatable process, you have an original work, and you cannot use repeatable solutions to solve quality problems.

Waste in the Process

Waste is defined as anything for which the customer is not willing to pay. An important part of repeatable products is reducing the waste that exists in the core process. Remember, the core process is creating the product. So, there is no need for anything that does not add value to the customer. You know it adds value for buyers when they are willing to pay for it. It means they value that thing more than money.

Lean

Lean is the standard methodology to eliminate waste. There are eight basic kinds of elements that make up the core process. The core process should be only the minimum required elements and anything else that the customer is not willing to pay for should be eliminated. These elements are:

1. Transport: Movement of products from one location to another. Transportation adds no value to the product.
2. Inventory: Products not being sold. Storing parts, pieces, and documentation before they are required.
3. Motion: Moving people or equipment more than needed. Only the movement that transforms the product in some manner is a value-added step.
4. Waiting: Interruptions or waiting for next step.
5. Overproduction: Producing more than is immediately demanded. Overproduction is the worst, as it ties up so many resources.
6. Over Processing: Extra steps or features not required by the customer, such as tighter tolerances or higher grade materials than are requested.
7. Defects: Inspecting and fixing errors.
8. Skills: Under-utilizing capabilities or delegating tasks with inadequate training.[52]

Original Work

Finished original work can be objectively well done or poorly done, but there is always a level of personal perspective. For example, a hamburger can be objectively good or bad if it differs from basic principles of composition and taste. But, a good hamburger can be created in many ways, depending on personal taste and design parameters. No two people will independently create the same original work and no one person will create each original work the same.

Over time, managing original work as repeatable work will always fail because the final product cannot be precisely defined in advance of producing the actual product, although original work can have general guidelines or goals. Before Toyota begins new designs, Toyota specifies the class of car, the target price, and the geographic demographics. The goals of the original work determine the direction and criteria, but original work cannot be documented and repeated. You will create a lot of waste when handling original work as repeatable work. Original work requires other methodologies.

Design Thinking

Design thinking is a methodology that reduces waste in solving original problems. Original problems are especially difficult or impossible to solve because of incomplete, contradictory, and changing requirements that are often difficult to recognize. Christoph Meinel and Larry Leifer assert that there are four principles to design thinking. The human rule: all design is social in nature. The ambiguity rule: design thinkers must preserve ambiguity. The redesign rule: all design is redesign. The tangibility rule: making ideas tangible always facilitates communication.[53]

Design thinking rules help reduce waste because original work requires working closely with a team that only knows what it wants when it has the final product. Design thinking means the team operates in ambiguity, should expect redesigns, and works in close collaboration with the entire group.

Software Development

Software development has made significant advances in recent years by recognizing that software is original and not standardizable. This wasn't always the case. In 1985, the US Department of Defense defined the waterfall software model, which treated software development as a repeatable process. The process was to document the requirements, design the solution, implement the solution, verify that the solution met the requirements, and finally maintain the system.

Agile software development is an improvement in software development because it recognizes and welcomes changing requirements, even late in development. Agile is a software development method that understood that over-reliance on processes, documentation, contract negotiation, and creating and following a plan resulted in dissatisfied customers and failed development projects.[54]

Scrum is a methodology similar to Agile, used to reduce waste in software development with rapidly changing requirements. Scrum software development progresses via a series of iterations (redesigns) called sprints, which last from one to four weeks. The goal at the end of each sprint is to have accomplished something tangible to facilitate communication. Development teams are social in nature and self-organizing. The teams are supported by a scrum master, whose role is similar to a coach, and the product owner, who is the voice of the customer.

Variability in Outputs

Modern organizations have environments that critically rely on information systems, which are a combination of original work and standardized work. Software developers are improving and changing the software, the operations staff is responsible for maintaining the systems and wants stability, and testers want to reduce the risk of failure.

DevOps

DevOps is a methodology that helps organizations reduce the variability in original work in information systems. DevOps is an organizational approach where building, testing, and releasing software can happen rapidly, frequently, and more reliably.[55]

DevOps' primary objective is to have the different interests work closer together to perform very frequent but small updates, which is a reconciliation of original work and standardized work. Frequent but small updates reduce risks because teams address bugs faster and can identify the last deployment that caused the error.

The Gang Analyzes Innovation Type 7—Core Process

Markus: Outsourced Development

Is your core process standardizable or original work?

> *My core process is original work. This description is very helpful. I have spent a lot of time trying to force my process to*

>be more like standardizable work. But, that is impossible, because we don't know what the solution looks like until we have it! This is a big load off my shoulders.

What methodology would help you improve quality?

>We use all the latest methods in design and software development.

Sarah: Interviewing Service

Is your core process standardizable or original work?

>My process is 100 percent standardizable. It is standardized assessment, which is valuable and comparable from one interview to the next.

What methodology would help you improve quality?

>The lean ideas will assist in making and developing our assessment on an ongoing basis.

Joko: Audio Algorithm

Is your core process standardizable or original work?

>My core process is original work. I don't even know what I can build on top of the algorithms or how users will use it.

What methodology would help you improve quality?

>I think in the future all of the methodologies you described will be helpful. But, for now all I need to do is work on improving the technology. I only need a small team right now because I don't want to spend any time trying to coordinate, I just want us to focus on building and improving the capabilities.

Enabling Process

Don't manage – lead change before you have to.
—Jack Welch

The enabling process sustains an organization and allows the team to perform its core process, which creates value. The enabling process includes cash management for a manufacturer, human resources for a software company, valet parking for restaurants, and scheduling for medical surgery. The enabling process is never the core aspect of an organization but is always critical to its success.

Persuasive management optimizes the enabling process and is the source of innovation. I won't spend significant time on the effective management of the enabling process because to include a portion of the management theories wouldn't do this field justice. There are many useful frameworks taught in MBA programs and published in thousands of books. But, I will examine the basic building blocks of what management is trying to do, as opposed to analyzing the various types of management practices. Peter Drucker has been described as "the inventor of modern management" and his groundbreaking work transformed modern management into a discipline now taught at business schools and practiced in companies all over the world. "Only three things happen naturally in organizations: friction, confusion, and underperformance," Drucker said. "Everything else requires leadership."

Effective management is a critical part of the enabling process, and its goal is to use as few resources as possible, but not any fewer than necessary. The things that happen naturally, friction, confusion, and underperformance, will demand more resources without offering more output. Active management is about constantly planning, organizing, staffing, directing, and controlling the factors of production to counterbalance the friction, confusion, and underperformance with harmony, clarity, and progress.

The factors of production are the resources required to create, launch, and sustain innovation.

Factor of Production	Description	Need
Capital	Tools and buildings	Low, Med, High
Land	Natural resources	Low, Med, High
Labor	Human efforts	Low, Med, High
Intellectual Property	Creations of the mind	Low, Med, High
Time	Duration of the process	Low, Med, High

Metrics

How do you know if you are managing resources well? You count and measure how you use the resources and how effective you are at using your selected types of funding. This system of measurement is metrics, and there are an infinite number of ways to count and measure performance. Metrics help you focus on something and let you know if you are improving or getting worse.

Thomas Monson is the leader of the Church of Jesus Christ of Latter-day Saints (Mormons), and he has instituted a culture of metrics across a worldwide organization. He has said, "When performance is measured, performance improves. When performance is measured and reported back, the rate of improvement accelerates." The Church has a lot of resources to measure and many funding sources. Church assets include land, capital, and intellectual property and are estimated to be worth about $40 billion, with zero debt. The church generates $8 billion in donations annually, which is more revenue than half of the Fortune 500 companies, the largest businesses in the United States. In the United States, the Church's income is tax-free, and the donations are usually tax-deductible for the donors. The church operates primarily through volunteer labor. The LDS Church has 15 million members worldwide and about 5 million members who volunteer between one and twenty hours a week to manage all operations at the local level. Five million volunteers mean the church "workforce" exceeds the combined number of employees of the two largest employers in the United States, Wal-Mart and the entire federal government. To provide some additional context, McDonald's employs 1.9 million worldwide at 37,000 restaurants. The LDS Church's 5 million weekly volunteers provide their service at 30,000 locations.

The LDS Church tracks metrics on every factor of production and every funding source. You should also track your most important metrics to measure and improve performance. Many startups track metrics that drive valuation, such as the growth in daily active users. Established companies track return on equity (ROE), the amount of profit they earn on invested capital. Most organizations track revenue and donations in many different forms and labor is measured as revenue per employee, average tenure, and by many other metrics.

No universal metric exists for the enabling process. Find metrics that measure the most important things and track them.

The Gang Analyzes Innovation Type 8—Enabling Process

Markus: Outsourced Development

What metrics will you use to monitor performance?

The most important metrics for me are those that show how profitable each project is. Revenue growth is important but most important is the profit we generate on each contract. I have had some small contracts make more money than larger contracts because large contracts require a lot more time and resources, so if the terms were messed up in the beginning, then it only damages the company the more work we do under that contract.

What resources are critical for your plan?

Factor of Production	Description	Need
Capital	Tools and building	Low
Land	Natural resources	Low
Labor	Human efforts	High
Intellectual Property	Creations of the mind	Med
Time	Duration of the process	Med

Sarah: Interviewing Service

What metrics will you use to monitor performance?

My focus will be on various revenue metrics. This is my bread and butter. It is all about the good leads and how we convert those leads into customers.

What resources are critical for your plan?

Factor of Production	Description	Need
Capital	Tools and building	Low
Land	Natural resources	Low
Labor	Human efforts	High
Intellectual Property	Creations of the mind	Medium
Time	Duration of the process	Medium

Joko: Audio Algorithm

What metrics will you use to monitor performance?

The most important metrics for me are about how many users are using the software and the amount of data we are able to process. Active users will drive valuation. The data we have will help improve the technology.

What resources are critical for your plan?

Factor of Production	Description	Need
Capital	Tools and building	Low
Land	Natural resources	Low
Labor	Human efforts	High
Intellectual Property	Creations of the mind	High
Time	Duration of the process	High

Economies of Scale

Quantity has a quality all its own.
—Joseph Stalin

Economies of scale means that the more you produce something, the less it costs to make each thing. It is the ninth type of innovation.

To illustrate economies of scale, imagine that FedEx had only one customer who needed to send a package overnight. The cost to deliver one package would be prohibitive. The costs for FedEx to deliver just one package from New York to San Francisco would include the cost of the airplane, the pilot, and the fuel. Of course, a lot of other overhead costs are in the mix but set them aside for a moment. A FedEx Boeing 757 costs about $9,000 an hour to fly and the flight time is six hours, so the cost to deliver one package would be $54,000.

Spending $54,000 on delivering one package is crazy. Fortunately, the price drops in half if you can deliver two. If you can manage to deliver ten packages, the price has decreased to $5,400. The cost per package continues to drop with each additional package you can fit on the plane. If you can fit 10,000 packages, the cost per package drops to $5.40. Economies of scale come from the relationship between the output and fixed cost. Fixed cost refers to the infrastructure you need to produce even one item, like the FedEx airplane. As production increases, your cost per unit continues to fall, just like the cost per package for FedEx.

Let's assume some simplistic revenue numbers to demonstrate the power of economies of scale. Assume that the average industry price for next day delivery is one hundred dollars. FedEx can charge one hundred dollars for each package and must have at least 540 on the airplane to break even on the $54,000 cost of flying. If FedEx can fill the plane with 10,000 packages, then it can generate revenue of $1 million with fixed costs of $54,000 and produce margins of $946,000 from one flight.

Economies of scale as a source of innovation can apply to more than just the product. FedEx's global size means the company has opportunities for other economies of scale. FedEx, for example, also has a channel economy of scale. In 2017 FedEx had 660 airplanes in operation around the world and moved 12 million shipments daily. FedEx also has a core process economy of scale because fuel purchased in bulk can reduce the cost per gallon, and the company has an enabling process economy of scale because it needs sophisticated logistics infrastructure to track the status and location of each package.

If you structure for scale before achieving scale, you will likely lose significant amounts of money. If FedEx ships fewer than 540 packages per flight then the organization is losing money on every flight.

Nobel Prize-winning economist Milton Friedman taught, "There is one and only one social responsibility of business—to use its resources and engage in activities designed to increase its profits so long as it stays within the rules of the game, which is to say, engages in open and free competition without deception or fraud." Observers who agree with Friedman will prematurely criticize economies-of-scale strategies precisely because in the beginning, they lose money. It appears to outsiders that the services are being subsidized by the government or by venture capital to deliver their services.

Even as the organization grows and is "successful" in pursuing product economy of scale, such as FedEx shipping more packages on each flight, the total company losses can still increase. FedEx would have ultimately failed if it tried to be as profitable as possible. FedEx had to achieve scale to other types of innovation, such as its channel, by acquiring more airplanes and more routes. As FedEx opens new routes and acquires new planes, each flight starts delivering 540 packages and the total losses have increased dramatically. It would appear that the bigger FedEx grows, the more money it loses. However, over time each flight increases the number of packages and margins increase. Ultimately, each flight achieves scale and carries 10,000 packages and generates $946,000 in margin.

Many other organizations benefit from economies of scale, especially in tech where fixed costs are high, the variable costs are low, and the demand can be global. Google search, Amazon, Facebook, EA Sports, Apple, and Microsoft all benefit from economies of scale.

The essential components are the price, fixed costs, variable cost per unit, and quantity. The algebraic expression is: $\pi = p*q - (Fn+wq)$ where:

- π is profit
- p is the sales price
- Fn is fixed costs
- w is variable cost per unit sold
- q is quantity sold

The Gang Analyzes Innovation Type 9—Economies of Scale

Markus: Outsourced Development

Describe your output.

Technically I would say the output is the completion of projects.

Describe your fixed costs.

Not a lot of fixed costs. Corporate office, sales team, accounting, IT, and other necessary infrastructure.

Describe your variable costs.

Biggest variable cost is the employee's or contractor's time to complete the project.

Do you have an opportunity for economies of scale?

I don't have economies-of-scale business. Of course, the answer is sort of. If I call the brand a fixed cost that takes years to build, then maybe. The bigger we grow then the more money we make. But, I wouldn't say it is a high fixed costs business where the more you sell, the more you make per unit. You make a little more, but it is just a little bit more.

Sarah: Interviewing Service

Describe your output.

My output is the interview assessment reports.

Describe your fixed costs.

I don't have a lot of fixed costs. They are primarily the enabling process, all the corporate structure and the original systems to receive calls, route them, and the original interview assessment.

Describe your variable costs.

I get to match revenue to most expenses. My variable costs are customer acquisition costs and interview costs.

Do you have an opportunity for economies of scale?

No, I don't think so.

Joko: Audio Algorithm

Describe your output.

The output is insight to spoken language and connection to other data. My software has learned to suggest a study guide based on the materials the professors would talk about in their lectures, including the inflections in their voices, compared to the exam questions and answers. The software suggests the most important sections from the textbooks and other reading materials. I have improved the algorithms over time and several people started using the software to study and get better grades.

Describe your fixed costs.

Software development is a huge fixed cost, especially to improve the software and take it to the highest output possible in other contexts.

Describe your variable costs.

Variable costs are just computing costs and they are very small compared to the fixed costs.

Do you have an opportunity for economies of scale?

Definitely I have an opportunity for economies of scale.

Culture

Our whole corporate culture is that we don't have a corporate culture.

—Erlich Bachman, *Silicon Valley*

The tenth type of innovation is culture. Culture is the attitude and behavior characteristics of a social group, and every group has its own. Culture is the way that the group sees the world. Often people see culture as artifacts of the social group, such as clothing, rituals, or language. But, Fons Trompenaars and Charles Hampden-Turner investigated deeper and conducted a large-scale survey of 8,841 managers and organization employees from 43 countries and developed Trompenaars' model of national culture differences.[56]

Culture is like water to a fish. Our culture surrounds us, so it's hard to recognize our own and to identify the differences between cultures. If you ask someone why he or she does something a particular way and the answer is "Why would I do it any other way?" that is culture. The cultural insights from Trompenaars will be helpful as you make decisions to craft a deliberate culture.

Trompenaars lists seven culture dimensions.
1. Universalists vs. Particularists
2. The Group vs. the Individual
3. Neutral vs. Emotional
4. Specific vs. Diffusive
5. Achievement vs. Ascription
6. Concepts of Time
7. Control vs. Environment

What is more important to you, rules or relationships?

Universalists vs. Particularists is the first cultural dimension. Universalists believe rules should be followed completely and apply to everyone everywhere. Particularists believe rules should be followed, but particular circumstances require exceptions and those particular personal relationships are more important than rules.

A universal culture establishes rules and then follows them, making no individual exceptions. You are a part of this culture when you believe there is one truth. As an organization, you have created and follow rules that are based on what is morally correct and to treat everyone the same regardless of status or position. If you set precedents in how you choose to deal with a unique circumstance with a team member, you apply the same decision to everyone in the group.

A particularist culture is the opposite. It recognizes changing circumstances and obligation to relationships are more important than rules because rules are more guiding teachings than rigid commandments. If you are part of this culture, then you understand that no one rule will work for all circumstances because they are always unique. If there is a high performer in the organization, you can't treat her like everyone else, so you make exceptions because you need her. Overall you treat everyone like family because that is how you want to be treated.

Do you prefer to work in a group or as an individual?

Groupists believe the group's efforts should be toward common goals and objectives. Individualists believe their efforts should be toward individual goals and they expect others to do the same.

Individual cultures are crafted around circumstances when people achieve alone and can accept personal responsibility. You believe that people's accomplishments are because they put in the effort and have the talent to succeed. Your favorite saying is "A camel is a horse designed by a committee" because group decisions always take too long and seem to mess things up.

Group cultures occur when people accomplish tasks together as a unit. You have seen that your team is successful only when you work together as a group. Sometimes getting everyone on the same page takes longer, but it is worth the time because when everyone is involved in the decision, you know there isn't anything you can't accomplish. You feel like a beehive, where everyone has a significant role, even if a single person's contribution seems small. You need everyone taking part for everything to function smoothly.

Do you display your emotions?

Neutralists believe that members of the group should not reveal feelings publicly. Emotionalists think group members should express their emotions immediately and openly.

If you are part of a neutral culture, then you know that people have strong emotions and reactions from time to time, but we should all be professional and well composed. You don't need others to make a scene when something goes well or poorly. There is no place for outbursts because you expect people to be in control of their behavior and emotions. Bringing strong emotions into the team just complicates the work you have to do.

Emotional cultures demonstrate their feelings by having an immediate outlet. This culture values communication through physical contact, dramatic facial expressions, and clear and sometimes strong language. When you meet friends and team members, you often give them hugs and tell each other how good it is to see each other. You celebrate successes together, and when you are upset you let people know by yelling, swearing, slamming doors, and occasionally throwing your pens or other items at a wall. You have thrown your phone a couple of times, but replacing them gets expensive, so you try to grab something else. You know we are all human, and we celebrate life together, both the good and the bad.

How separate do you keep your private and working life?

Specificists believe social or work relationships should be contained to the specific domain. In other words, work friends are compartmentalized with work friends, and family friends are compartmentalized as family friends. Diffusivists believe any personal relationships should spread to all your other personal relationships, regardless of origin.

These two types of cultures are created when individuals maintain separation between personal and work or whether they allow the relationships to spread to many or all other areas of life.

If you are a specificist, then you have a family, school friends, work friends, church friends, and sports friends but none of them know each other. There is no reason why the people you work with would come to church with you. You held a party once and invited friends from different circles, and it was weird because no one had anything in common, except just knowing you.

If you are a diffusivist then all the people you know all know each other. For you, when someone becomes a friend they become a part of your life. Your friends at work helped organize your niece's baptism because your work friends know how important the baptism was for your aging parents to feel connected to your brother and his daughter now that they moved to England.

Do you have to prove yourself to receive status or is it given to you?

Achievement vs. Ascription is the fifth culture dimension. Every culture grants a higher status to some members of the group. Those with higher status receive extra scrutiny from other members. Some cultures grant status based on member achievements and other cultures ascribe status to individuals with age, class, education, tenure, gender, and race.

As a part of an ascribed culture, you appreciate that those with a high status accept the responsibility they have been given. You can see that all the leadership is "old white males," but the criticism is off-base. What the leaders contribute to the organization is decades of experience in many different roles. They were educated at some of the most prestigious universities in the world. Most of the leadership has some family connections, often going back generations, but what it means to you is they have had a lot of mentorship and access to previous leadership that others just don't have. The organization is too critical to be left to someone without that context and exposure to the history of the organization.

Achievement cultures grant a higher status to individuals based on how well they perform in the role. You love being a part of achievement cultures. Everyone has the same opportunity to rise through the ranks of the organization based on how well they perform. Some move fast, and others move slowly. As you look at the leadership, you see many different races and cultures, both men and women, and PhDs working alongside some college and high school drop-outs. You know you will be successful here because you have the same opportunities as everyone else.

Organizations can cycle from ascription to achievement cultures. To motivate better performance, an organization rewards higher achieving individuals and grants them positions of status. As a result of this focus, the culture moves toward achievement. The most recent performance is weighted highly, but some members who have achieved higher status are unable to maintain their recent performance. As a result of their failures, the organization will move toward ascription to respect what people achieve based on length of experience. The shift to ascription slows performance and does not grant high-status to higher performers, and so the organization creates a cycle.

Do you do things one at a time or several things at once?

Sequential and synchronic cultures feel differently about their relationships with the passage of time. Sequentialists see events occurring in a timeline and happening in order. Your meetings are planned in advance, with an established agenda, have a start and end time, and you keep to the schedule. For you, "time is money," and time is the only resource you can never get back, so you get the most out of your work day and your free time. You have no patience for people who are unprepared and waste your time; it shows a complete lack of respect.

Synchronic culture views events happening in the past, present, and future as related. You often work on several projects at once, and view plans and commitments as flexible. Life, nature and your team all have a rhythm, and it is important to follow that rhythm. Your work today is a result of the pace and the work from yesterday just as tomorrow will come from the rhythm today.

Organizations will also measure the present, the past, and the future at different intervals. If you focus on multi-year contracts, you will measure differently than an organization with an annual government budget cycle, or one that operates on a monthly billing cycle, and even differently than one that runs on a daily news cycle.

Do you control your environment or does your environment control you?

A control culture believes individuals are in control of their environment. Environment cultures believe that individuals just operate inside what the environment controls.

If you suspect that you are in control of the environment you will behave in a much more confident manner because you expect your actions to dictate events. For example, if you feel in control of the industry niche in which you operate you will react with conviction when faced with conflict and resistance, even from customers. You will see this as a strength because you are imposing a better way to the environment.

If you sense you are just a player in the environment and subject to the movements of the system then you respond to the tendencies of customers by adapting. You see these signals as indicators for change. You are comfortable with being adaptable, and this is a virtue.

The Gang Analyzes Innovation Type 10—Culture

Markus: Outsourced Development

What is more important to you, rules or relationships?

Relationships are more important to me.

Do you prefer to work in a group or as an individual?

I prefer to work in a team. I do my best work on small iterations where we each work on something and then bring it back to the group. Most projects are built collaboratively with each person working on their piece, but it all has to fit together smoothly.

Do you display your emotions?

Yes, I show my emotions all the time. I am who I am, and my work is an expression of my personality and vision of what I contribute to the world. I need my emotions to be close so that I can create.

How separate do you keep your private and working life?

> *I like having a small circle of close friends. I like being close to the people I work with, but I don't usually have them come over to my house. I enjoy having a close culture, but I don't think they need to get involved in my personal life.*

Do you have to prove yourself to receive status or is it given to you?

> *I think it is a combination of both. I like getting recognized for testing myself, but I also like the status for achieving certain things. I don't think I have to prove myself each time because my work requires inspiration and it doesn't always happen at the highest level each time.*

Do you do things one at a time or several things at once?

> *I have to do several things at once. My projects have a lot of moving parts that I have to stay on top of all at once. Plus, when I am stuck on something creatively it helps me to work on something else and then come back to it. I can't force a good idea, but if I give it some time, then it will come on its own.*

Do you control your environment or does your environment control you?

> *I think the setting controls me. I am just along for the ride and I try to do the best with whatever comes along.*

Sarah: Interviewing Service

What is more important to you, rules or relationships?

> *Relationships. I love top performers, and I treat people I work with like family.*

Do you prefer to work in a group or as an individual?

> *I prefer to work as an individual. I like when I work with people that are good at what they do and can specialize in their domain.*

Do you display your emotions?

> *I am not emotional, except when I am pissed off or excited and happy.*

How separate do you keep your private and working life?

> *I completely mix the two. My best friends are my coworkers, and I like to recruit my friends to come and work with me.*

Do you have to prove yourself to receive status or is it given to you?

> *I want to prove myself every day. I want those I work with to show themselves. I have had to fire some people with fantastic experience, but if they don't perform, there is no room for them.*

Do you do things one at a time or several things at once?

> *I do one thing at a time. I prefer to be laser focused on something and to do well on that thing and then to move on to the next.*

Do you control your environment or does your environment control you?

> *I think you control your environment—but you need to pick the situation you know you can control.*

Joko: Audio Algorithm

What is more important to you, rules or relationships?

> *Rules are more important to me. I want to find truth and how things are designed to operate and then follow those guidelines to achieve the desired result.*

Do you prefer to work in a group or as individual?

> *It depends on the type of work. Usually I prefer to work alone because I can produce the best code when I am at home alone. But, I know that I have to work with other people to get other things done.*

Do you display your emotions?

> *Not really. I prefer to keep these things to myself.*

How separate do you keep your private and working life?

> *I usually keep things separate. I like to have different aspects of my life.*

Do you have to prove yourself to receive status or is it given to you?

> *I think you have to prove yourself. Technology changes quickly, so you have to keep up or be left behind.*

Do you do things one at a time or several things at once?

I do best when I can focus in on one thing for days or weeks at a time.

Do you control your environment or does your environment control you?

I think we are all just going with the flow of whatever life brings us. I think we can choose how we react, but even our reactions, choices, and preferences were all dictated by an environment that we can't control. I am just the result of an environment I didn't choose.

Governance

L'Etat, c'est moi.
—Louis XIV

Governance is the practice of controlling an entity and exists when two or more people coordinate and organize to accomplish something. As a theoretical concept, governance is inevitable in any social organization or coordination. A an easily remembered description of the rules of governance is found in the 1992 movie *Aladdin.* Jafar is the villain and he persuades the poor and imprisoned hero, Aladdin, to find the genie's lamp. "You've heard of the golden rule, haven't you? Whoever has the gold makes the rules!"

In *The Dictator's Handbook: Why Bad Behavior Is Almost Always Good Politics,* authors Bruce Bueno de Mesquita and Alastair Smith provide more detailed insight about grabbing and maintaining power. To govern effectively, you need to rely on as few people as possible and still maintain a pool of replacements who are capable of replacing them if they create problems. You need to control the flow of money and reward your supporters just enough to keep them loyal.

When you look at any organization of people, divide up those involved into three groups: the interchangeables are those who have a voice in selecting the leader, the influentials are those who actually select the leader, and the essentials are those whose support will mean victory.

This can be a little confusing at first, so let me give you an example. Imagine you are a startup founder of a tech company. You need a few co-founders you trust who complement your skill set and who will be critical to your success. You pay them well enough and give them some ownership in the company. These co-founders are your essentials. As your company grows you hire a group of influentials to perform under the direction of your co-founders. This second group is important because they might be needed to replace the positions filled by your co-founders, so you pay them well and give them some equity, but not as much as you gave the co-founders. The influentials hire interchangeables to work under their direction. The work of the interchangeables requires expertise, but they can be replaced by another person in the job market with the same skill set. This group is important because from this pool will come your next generation of influentials. You pay interchangeables a market salary and give them market equity.

I have seen founders violate the rules that promote effective governance. They have relied on too many essentials, have not had enough replacements, have not controlled the flow of money, or have not compensated their supporters adequately. Founders with too many essentials have too many interests. As a result, I have seen, essentials leave to form their own competing startup, or form internal alliances to compete against other essentials, or remove the founder. Founders who do not cultivate a group of influentials to replace the essentials remove the option and leverage of replacing their essentials. I have seen essentials with too much power because they become irreplaceable, and I have seen startups struggle to survive when the essential does leave, because no one is ready to step in and fill the role. When founders can't generate revenue in the long run they can't control their own destiny. When founders don't reward everyone with increasing valuations they don't have the critical tool to govern. When founders offer too little equity to their co-founders, they offer betrayal instead of trust.

These rules of effective governance apply in other coordination activities outside of a hierarchy. You need funding for your startup, so you raise money from venture capitalists (VCs). You find a VC who understands your market and technology and is willing to anchor your first round of funding. This VC is essential to your funding and helps bring in other investors. Without this first VC, you would raise nothing so you cultivate this relationship and give him board representation. Other VC firms invest in your company and are part of your influential investors along with a few interchangeable wealthy individuals. Over time you work on building trust with them by increasing the valuation of their investment. You know they are all capable of a much larger investment in the future.

Working with customers also follows the same governance rules: Rely on a few customers that generate good margins, maintain a large customer base for revenue and margin stability, and continue to provide value with your product while charging enough to keep them loyal. Violate these rules with customers and you will risk losing the ability to govern. If the relative value you provide decreases and you lose the essential customer, you lose control over the flow of revenue. Governance is a type of innovation because it is critical to the organization. There will always be multiple methods of improving and working toward effective governance. The innovator will apply these rules in the hierarchy, funding sources, customers, and channels.

The Gang Analyzes Innovation Type 11—Governance

Markus: Outsourced Development

> Who are the essentials you need in your hierarchy?
>> *I need management to help me in the operations of the various pieces of the business. I want to grow a business based on the work that I do; I don't want to manage a growing business.*
>
> How will you apply the rules of governance?
>> *The clients we work with and the prices they are willing to pay dictate the level of talent in the market that we can hire to work with us. We can't hire the most talented people unless we are working with the clients with the largest budgets and who demand the highest quality. I will need to cultivate some essential clients so that I can manage the revenue in my organization to get the influentials I need.*

Sarah: Interviewing Service

> Who are the essentials you need in your hierarchy?
>> *I know that I will need to raise some money so those are the essentials. I will give some equity to other team members, but I want to be in charge in the company. I am good at managing*

people, and I add the most value in the company because I can sell, and at the end of the day, these are the two most important qualities in the hierarchy. I can govern from the top and make sure that the organization is well run and people are getting their work done. So everyone else I see as influentials, not as essentials.

How will you apply the rules of governance?

I see the largest risk of not being able to control my own destiny in the revenue. I think there is a risk of gaining one essential customer early in the process. While that is great for revenue we would customize the experience to that customer, because their revenue is so important. That influence on our product will put the entire organization at risk if we lose that customer. I will need to make sure that I add smaller interchangeable customers.

Joko: Audio Algorithm

Who are the essentials you need in your hierarchy?

I need someone to help guide me in navigating the commercialization of the software. I know it works for students, but I don't know what other applications it will have or how to sell it.

How will you apply the rules of governance?

I don't think I need to be concerned too much in the beginning because the most important thing is the technology. However, I am afraid that over time the highest bidder will decide how it is applied. For example, I don't want the technology to be used for spying on political opponents, even though that might be very lucrative. We also will need to be careful about our partners because if we incorporate other technology it might limit what customers we can serve or it might make us lazy in developing our own technology.

Customer Engagement and Service

Customer service and customer support is not something you do; it is the result of everything you do. If you want to influence customers in a particular way, you must have harmony between every type of innovation. Customer service is the twelfth type of innovation and is a blend of all other types.

To illustrate the concept, let's examine Amazon. The first step, as described by founder Jeff Bezos on the company website, is to start with a vision of what you want to accomplish for your customers.

> *We see our customers as invited guests to a party, and we are the hosts. It's our job every day to make every important aspect of the customer experience a little bit better.*

Below are charts of each innovation type, with a quote from Bezos setting the expectations for Amazon in that area. To the right is how that expectation is put into practice and the effect on customer service.

Innovation Type	Jeff Bezos Quote on Amazon Expectations	Amazon Practice that Impacts Customer Service
Product: Relative Advantage	"Real estate is the key cost of physical retailers. That's why there's the old saw: location, location, location."	Provide selection and service at prices that is impossible for physical stores store to offer because of the site costs of physical retailers.
Product: Observability	"Advertising is the price you pay for having an unremarkable product or service."	The world's largest online seller delivers packages in brown boxes with the Amazon logo, which provides an opportunity for neighborhoods to observe deliveries from Amazon services.
Product: Trialability	"Amazon.com strives to be the e-commerce destination where consumers can find and discover anything they want to buy online."	Amazon provides an easy 30-day return policy, or if the customer misses that deadline the customer can sell the item to other users through Amazon.com.
Product: Compatibility	"There are two ways to extend a business. Take inventory of what you're good at and extend out from your skills. Or determine what your customers need and work backward, even if it requires learning new skills. Kindle is an example of working backward."	When the world's largest bookseller produces an electronic reader, the device is compatible with e-books purchased through Amazon and the customer can browse and purchase devices directly from the device.
Product: Complexity	"The best customer service is if the customer doesn't need to call you, doesn't	One-Click Ordering is a hallmark of Amazon services. Order and check out in one click.

Innovation Type	Jeff Bezos Quote on Amazon Expectations	Amazon Practice that Impacts Customer Service
	need to talk to you. It just works."	
Product: Buyer Motivation	"You don't want to negotiate the price of simple things you buy every day."	Amazon allows customers to get what they need quickly, save money and time, ensure that they get the lowest price possible, and even use the platform to sell their products.
Funding	"Your margin is my opportunity."	Amazon does not try to maximize the margin on every sale but is content to sell more at small margins.
Info	"We use high-performance transactions systems, complex rendering and object caching, workflow and queuing systems, business intelligence and data analytics, machine learning and pattern recognition, neural networks and probabilistic decision making, and a wide variety of other techniques."	Amazon uses information to provide personalized shopping recommendations for customers. Also, Amazon developed and used an anticipatory shipping model for predicting when you are likely to purchase particular products and sends the items to a local distribution center, so the items will be ready for shipping when you order them.
Brand	"If you do build a great experience, customers tell each other about that. Word of mouth is very powerful."	Amazon's brand remains powerful because it delivers on customer expectations due to its advanced scale and core processes.

Innovation Type	Jeff Bezos Quote on Amazon Expectations	Amazon Practice that Impacts Customer Service
Channel	"In the old world, you devoted 30 percent of your time to building a great service and 70 percent of your time to shouting about it. In the new world, that inverts."	Marketing: Amazon spends $1.35B on online search advertising. Sales: Amazon accounts for 60 percent of online sales growth in 2015 and 31 percent of online holiday shopping in 2016
Network	"Many characterized AWS as a bold—and unusual—bet when we started. 'What does this have to do with selling books?' We could have stuck to the knitting. I'm glad we didn't. Or did we? Maybe the knitting has as much to do with our approach as the arena."	Amazon Web Services (AWS), offers a suite of cloud-computing services that make up an on-demand computing platform. AWS generates $10B in annual revenue and $2.4B in operating income. Network is closed and compatible.
Core Process	"We will take all the capacity that the U.S. Postal Service can give us and that UPS can give us and we still need to supplement it."	Amazon now leases 40 jets and has purchased 4,000 truck trailers to improve speed and delivery to customers.
Enabling Process	"As I meet with teams across Amazon, I am continually amazed at the passion, intelligence, and creativity on display."	AWS, Marketplace, and Prime are all autonomous services that employees have created to leverage existing Amazon capabilities. Amazon customers embrace each service.

Innovation Type	Jeff Bezos Quote on Amazon Expectations	Amazon Practice that Impacts Customer Service
Economies of Scale	"On the Internet, companies are scale businesses, characterized by high fixed costs and relatively low variable costs. You can be two sizes: You can be big, or you can be small."	Amazon is using economies of scale to a significant advantage in selling and recommending products, logistics to provide near immediate service, and IT infrastructure with AWS.
Culture	"My own view is that every company requires a long-term view."	Many Internet companies and public companies focus on short-term results. Amazon believes building for the future benefits the customers.
Governance	"If the company does a good job for customers and the long term does a good job for shareholders, then that's the best investor relations."	Jeff Bezos founded Amazon.com in 1994.

The Gang Analyzes Innovation Type 12—Customer Service

Markus: Outsourced Development

What is your vision for customer service?

I want to be a close partner with customers where we work on mission-critical projects.

Review your analysis in the other types. Do you need to make any changes to your vision or your other types?

I need to improve our contract, on-boarding, and project-management process to better serve our clients.

Sarah: Interviewing Service

What is your vision for customer service?

I think the key is what I want the brand impression to be. The impression I want people to have with my brand is that they have a partner in the job search. I want my customers to feel like this isn't just a transaction, but that we care about them and like we are part of their team while they are searching. I want them not to feel alone.

Review your analysis in the other types. Do you need to make any changes to your vision or your other types?

No, I don't think so.

Joko: Audio Algorithm

What is your vision for customer service?

I don't want any interaction with customers. I want the technology to just work for them so they have no reason to contact me.

Review your analysis in the other types. Do you need to make any changes to your vision or to your other types?

No, I don't need to make any changes.

Complex Coordination

The final type of innovation is complex coordination. The term was popularized by Peter Thiel, cofounder of PayPal and the $2 billion venture capital firm Founders Fund. The Founders Fund has identified an innovation strategy that involves "large-scale complex coordination, getting a lot of different pieces together to work."[57] [58] Thiel stated, "My PayPal colleague Elon Musk started both SpaceX and Tesla, which are extremely charismatic businesses, because it involved somewhat larger-scale complex coordination, getting a lot of different pieces together to work."

Thiel has given other examples of successful complex coordination strategies. Regarding iPhone and Apple, he states that their success was due to "getting all these different pieces coordinated in just the right way. That included the incredible complexity of the manufacturing process set-up, the distribution, [and] marketing coordinated in just the right way. For some reason, that's quite hard to do."[59]

Mixing Types of Innovation

Tesla engages in complex coordination. Tesla is the first American car company to go public since Ford Motor Company in 1956. It is an organization that has some of the country's finest innovation strategy, product development, internal operations, commercialization, and positioning for future growth.

The foundational piece of Tesla's innovation is its product, as it manufactures a quality electric car. Tesla's Model S P85D rated a 103 out of 100 from Consumer Reports in 2015. "It kind of broke the system," says Jake Fisher, director of the magazine's auto test division.[60]

Tesla's technology is so good the company can pursue revenue sources outside of its core line by licensing technology to other car companies. Thiel claims, "Daimler uses Tesla's battery packs; Mercedes-Benz uses a Tesla powertrain; Toyota uses a Tesla motor.

General Motors has even created a task force to track Tesla's next moves."[61]

Tesla's use of information also gives it an advantage. It collects information each second the car is driven and all charging data from each of its vehicles and transmits this to corporate headquarters. Centralizing the data has created a quality feedback loop to improve all aspects of the product.

This is not all. Tesla innovates in its core process and has made improvements to the manufacturing process, and established a culture and mentality unique to the automobile industry.[62] Tesla has innovated in governance by appointing a part-time CEO, who took the job at the age of 37, with no previous automobile experience. Tesla innovates in its channel by developing its direct sales network, bypassing the industry standard dealerships and their business model of servicing cars as a profit center.[63]

Executing well in one or two areas is rare and is usually enough to establish lasting differentiation. But combining so many pieces as Tesla has done compounds the effects. Brian Singerman, a partner at Founders Fund and creator of iGoogle, discussed the merits of complex coordination. "It is extremely difficult, if not impossible, to clone these types of businesses with two guys in a garage. This is not something that you can hack up in a couple of months."[64]

The Gang Analyzes Innovation Type 13—Complex Coordination

What combinations of types and grades of innovation would strengthen your idea?

Markus: Outsourced Development

> *I don't want to try complex coordination. All I need to do is create an industry standard business.*

Sarah: Interviewing Service

> *I don't think that any complex coordination is possible with my idea and the way that I work.*

Joko: Audio Algorithm

> *This is an interesting concept. I have just thought that the product would be all that I need to worry about. But I think the most important types are the product, information, brand, and hierarchy. I will need to carefully manage these other aspects with the product.*

PART 4: PEOPLE

These chapters are about who needs to be on the innovation team and their roles. Jim Collins, the author of *Good to Great*, calls this "the bus." You are the bus driver and you "start by getting the right people on the bus, the wrong people off the bus, and the right people in the right seats."[65]

You need a diversely talented team to be successful with innovation in the long run. Breaking constraints and managing the resulting disorder demands team members have at least the minimum amount of expertise and sufficient motivation. Additionally, teams need a mixture of creatives to break constraints, systematics to manage the disorder, and bureaucrats to maintain the new process. When people are in the wrong seats, the resulting problems are predictable, but fixable.

Expertise and Motivation

In some parts of life, like mathematics and science, yeah, I was a genius. I would top all the top scores you could ever measure it by.
—Steve Wozniak

As you start looking around for people to join your team, you need at the minimum the right skills and sufficient motivation to execute the idea. These concepts are evident in theory, but much more nuanced in practice. If a prospective team member does not meet these two criteria, do NOT add them to the team. No matter how much you like them or how long you have known them or to whom they are related.

Everything built in the world has come from humans and is the result of innovation. Machines designed and manufactured by people carry much of the workload: airplanes, automobiles, computers, washing machines, dishwashers, ovens, microwaves, and blenders. Innovation does not happen without people, and when people don't accomplish a possible task, it is because they don't want to or they don't have the skill to do so.

Charlie Munger, vice chairman of Berkshire Hathaway and close friend of Warren Buffett, has given the following apocryphal story about the German physicist Max Planck. After winning the Nobel Prize, Planck went around Germany giving speeches. His chauffeur heard the talk so many times that he knew it by heart, and so one time, he asked Max Planck if he could give the address. Planck agreed, they changed places, and the lecture came off famously. But then came the Q&A, with the very first question being one that the chauffeur had no hope of answering. The driver replied: "I'm surprised to hear such an elementary question on high energy physics here in Munich. It's so simple, I'll let my chauffeur answer it."

This story demonstrates the kind of superficial knowledge that the chauffeur had and the deep understanding that Planck had. Building a team requires judgment to find the right balance between theoretical knowledge, firsthand experience in similar situations, and raw capacity. Work backward from the constraints you are trying to break to determine what expertise you need on your team.

Next, you have to put in the work and the effort. If you are lazy and unreliable, nothing else about your capabilities matters. The world is always changing, so you need to put in the effort. Elon Musk provided the following advice to entrepreneurs.

> *You have to put in 80-hour to 100-hour weeks every week. If other people are putting in 40-hour work weeks and you are putting in 100-hour work weeks, then even if you are doing the same thing, you will achieve in four months what it takes them a year to achieve.*[66]

Finding and sustaining the motivation to pursue hard things is not easy. To continue, evaluate your motivations and use them to propel you to continue when it is appropriate.

Intrinsic motivation comes from within the individual to accomplish something that is worth doing, regardless of the outcome. This type of motivation comes from the work itself, from the purpose of the work, or from personal goals.

If you are motivated by the outcome of doing something, this is extrinsic motivation. The most common extrinsic motivations are competition and the desire to beat others, fear of disappointing someone else, desire for rewards or to avoid punishment, or from inertia (you did it before, so you continue to do it now).

Be honest with yourself about your motivations because this will help you evaluate when to continue and when to give up. It is challenging and stressful to continue in a cause when it appears more and more likely that failure is inevitable, but persistence is present in every successful team. However, not all teams that are persistent will win.

Most people give up when faced with adversity, but when it comes to innovation, failure is always the most likely outcome.

The Gang Analyzes Expertise and Motivations

Markus: Outsourced Development

What expertise is required for your idea?

I need designers and software developers.

Give one or more examples of extrinsic motivation for your idea.

Some people are driven to collect accolades and public recognition. Also, some people are always in search of the quick payday and the project that they can do quickly.

Give one or more examples of intrinsic motivation for your idea.

For me, I like to create beautiful and useful things. For example, I paint during the weekends, and every few months I will have a show at an art gallery. I don't do it for the money or to become famous. I do it because I like to see my creations in the world and to see them appreciated by other people.

Sarah: Interviewing Service

What expertise is required for your idea?

My idea depends on being able to generate the sales channels and sell the product, it requires expertise in creating the interview assessments, the technical skills to manage the phone calls and the back-end system for those conducting the interviews to record their notes to send to the client.

Give one or more examples of extrinsic motivation for your idea.

Making money motivates me. I like to earn money, and this idea can be huge, measured by revenue and in valuation. This is a startup idea that is scalable and can be sustained by revenue. It is a real business.

Give one or more examples of intrinsic motivation for your idea.

I want to help job-seekers improve their interview skills to express clearly who they are. It sincerely bothers me when candidates and companies use a misleading interview to assess a good match.

Joko: Audio Algorithm

What expertise is required for your idea?

Overall for my entire vision, you need expertise in natural language processing, machine learning, linear algebra, calculus, probability and statistics, and neurology, neuroplasticity, and the human brain.

Give one or more examples of extrinsic motivation for your idea.

Some people are driven by money or fame. I am afraid some people are motivated by infamy.

Give one or more examples of intrinsic motivation for your idea.

I know this is an over-used motivation, but I want technology to improve the world. Most people in the world just want to live a happy life and technology is the key to improving the living conditions and the lives of millions of people around the world.

Creatives

> *Creativity is just connecting things. When you ask creative people how they did something, they feel a little guilty because they didn't really do it, they just saw something. It seemed obvious to them after a while.*
> —Steve Jobs

Creatives are naturally attracted to original work. Each original work result is unique, and creatives enjoy the process of discovery inherent in original work.

If you consider yourself a creative, I want you to come away with this idea: You are difficult to work with, and when you produce the best results you are disruptive.

If you are not a creative, I want you to come away with this idea: You might not understand creatives, but they are critical to innovation. To get the best out of creatives, create an environment that helps them do their best work.

Original problems are particularly challenging or impossible to solve because of incomplete, contradictory, and changing requirements that are often difficult to recognize. Creatives love these types of problems because they enjoy unlocking the puzzle for the finished result.

In the 2003 book *Leading Geeks*, Paul Glen addresses creatives and original work in the domain of the computer sciences but the ideas apply to any area. Glen writes that, with technical work, failure is standard precisely because the work is ambiguous. The final result and the path to get there are unclear, so the odds of failure are high. It is possible you only know that you are wrong once you get to the end. As a result, figuring out what to do can be harder than doing it.

Creatives are incredibly difficult to manage. The work is hard to define when it is complete, the process is even harder to explain, and the progress is irregular, with bursts of productivity and extended periods of slow growth. Eric Schmidt, former CEO of Google and current chairman of Alphabet, wrote about creatives in his book *How Google Works*:

> *It is also why they are uniquely difficult to manage, especially under old models, because no matter how hard you try, you can't tell people like that how to think. If you can't tell someone how to think, then you have to learn to manage the environment where they think. And make it a place where they want to come every day.*[67]

Creatives must be nonconformists because they are changing the systems around them and by definition, most people conform to their systems. The background of many creatives is usually nontraditional as a result of or causing their nonconformist attitudes. They are in one way or another an outsider to traditional social groups, due to their age, country of origin, or educational background. In the study *America's New Immigrant Entrepreneurs: Then and Now,* researchers analyzed 335 engineering and technology startups and found that in Silicon Valley 43.9 percent of the startups were founded by at least one immigrant. Each younger generation also has an opportunity to approach original work without being anchored to the solutions of the prior generation.

Creatives don't conform to most social conventions and need long periods of concentration and isolation to perform their best work. Isolation pulls creatives away from conventional thinking and allows them to focus intensely, to iterate quickly and to form new mental connections.

Creatives are a required component of innovation because they break through the current constraints that others have been unable to understand. Most people are not pure creatives. Most people by definition are like each other and are conformists. Most people avoid the risks of original work: ambiguity and failure.

The Gang Analyzes Creatives

What is the role for a creative in your idea?

Markus: Outsourced Development

Creatives are the most important piece of my idea. Essentially my idea is outsourced original work. Since this type of work is difficult for people to manage in their organizations, they turn to us to develop the solutions they need.

Sarah: Interviewing Service

I need creatives for crafting the technical solutions and the interview assessments. Those things right now are "original work" that we need to solve. I don't need creatives once we are up and running.

Joko: Audio Algorithm

We are working to solve something that has never been done before, so all the work is original and we need a lot of creatives. I have seen some people with the required expertise, but they are actually just bureaucrats, people who can only do what they are told.

Supporting Roles

> *Sometimes it is the people no one imagines anything of, who do the things that no one can imagine.*
> —Alan Turing

Innovation teams need to be balanced. Creatives can break pre-existing constraints, but they cannot organize the facilitating environment or the resulting chaos. Creatives need a team of systematics to bring order to innovation and bureaucrats to sustain it.

Systematics are creators, similar to creatives. But systematics don't create original work; they create organization and structure for standardizable and repeatable work. Bureaucrats don't and can't create; they execute on existing processes for repeatable work.

Systematics

Systematics have a vision of how all the pieces work together and how they should work together. Without systematics, innovations die.

If a team is made of only creatives, then chaos reigns unbridled. Karen Martin, an author and business consultant and systematic, wrote: "Chaos is the enemy of any organization that strives to be outstanding."[68]

A systematic's approach is to identify a problem and then to work back to determine the steps to design or redesign a system that can produce a result without the problem. Systematics identify all the steps in the process and the key controls and any other relevant information. Systematics obtain an empathetic understanding of the individuals involved in the process and how changes will affect people. Armed with this information a systematic can develop the standard operating procedures and document the steps to create order from the chaos of innovation.

A systematic's goal is to hand off the designed system to be managed by bureaucrats without new systematic or creative influence. Accordingly, the parts of the plan include:

1. Authority: Team members need to know who has authority to make decisions. The systematic defines the hierarchy. To whom does the bureaucrat report?
2. Rules: Team members need to know what the parameters are for the process. The systematic defines these rules, such as the experience and education required to complete the tasks and when exceptions should be referred up the hierarchy.
3. Task: Team members need to know what they are expected to do. The systematic defines the tasks that are to be done and by whom at each stage of the hierarchy and for each step in the process.
4. Judgment: Not all scenarios can be defined explicitly in the rules and will require judgment. The systematic determines the experience that is necessary and delegated to each level of the hierarchy to complete the tasks.

Bureaucrats

Bureaucrats execute their role in the environment designed by the systematics. A bureaucrat is and should be more concerned with procedural correctness than with people or even with the purpose of the procedure. Without bureaucrats, innovations die.

German sociologist Max Weber defined a bureaucratic as one who:[69]

- Exercises the authority delegated to him by impersonal rules, and his loyalty is enlisted on behalf of the faithful execution of his official duties.
- Work is rewarded by a regular salary and prospects of advancement in a lifetime career.
- Must exercise his judgment and his skills, but his duty is to place these at the service of a higher authority. Ultimately he is responsible only for the impartial execution of assigned tasks and must sacrifice his personal judgment if it runs counter to his official duties.
- Bureaucratic control is the use of rules, regulations, and formal authority to guide performance. It includes such things as budgets, statistical reports, and performance appraisals to regulate behavior and results.

Bureaucracy carries a negative connotation of excessive regulation and impersonal service in conforming to rules that delay the thing they are trying to accomplish. Creatives lament the bureaucracy that is the result of their original work, especially when the creatives have to manage it.

Bureaucrats believe familiar things like "Just tell me what to do, and I will do it," "If it ain't broke, don't fix it," and "But we've always done it this way." Bureaucrats should believe these things because change produces disorder and their role is just to execute. Do not expect more from them, although they may be capable of producing original work or new systems since they are closest to the problems. But often they don't have the context to understand the implications of their recommendations, which would create more chaos than would be solved by their solution.

The Gang Analyzes Supporting Roles

Markus: Outsourced Development

What is the role for a systematic in your idea?

With so many creatives we need a systematic to help us manage the process, deliverables, communication with the customer, and billing and collections.

What is the role for a bureaucrat in your idea?

I want to share assistants with the creative staff to make them more productive. There are a lot of tasks, such as time tracking, expense reports, travel, and status updates that I don't think creatives like doing or do well. We can have a systematic define the workflow and then we just need some bureaucrats to help us execute.

Sarah: Interviewing Service

What is the role for a systematic in your idea?

I need systematics to create the internal processes to manage.

What is the role for a bureaucrat in your idea?

> Most of the work once I have a working solution will be done by "bureaucrats," such as sales, the interviewers, and maintaining all the internal processes.

Joko: Audio Algorithm

What is the role for a systematic in your idea?

> I think a systematic is helpful to make things more useful for an end-user. Usually, I am so focused on solving a technical problem that it is hard for me to empathize with an end-user.

What is the role for a bureaucrat in your idea?

> I don't know if there is a role for a bureaucrat for some time. I don't like to work with people who can only do what they have been told. It is frustrating.

Mismatched Roles

Whatever you are, be a good one.
—Abraham Lincoln

Over time only a diverse team of technical talents and abilities can be successful. Teams need a mixture of creatives to break constraints, systematics to manage the disorder, and bureaucrats to maintain the new process. Remember, you are the bus driver and you "start by getting the right people on the bus, the wrong people off the bus, and the right people in the right seats."

You need to keep your team balanced, or you risk messing up the chemistry. If you have too many bureaucrats, Marc Andreessen warns, the team will "end up with a staff that only knows how to be a big company — that only knows how to maintain something that someone else has already built — which is death in any industry where things change all the time."[70]

If you have too many creatives, your team can't stay focused because creatives will always have an idea on how to improve the product. Remember, original work cannot define itself until the finished product is complete. Creatives never see the product as complete! Too many of them can't stay focused and will be in a constant cycle of improving the product.

If you have too many systematics, they will strangle everything and prevent you from moving fast. Systematics want to create systems for everything that is chaotic. Innovation is inherently chaotic and messy, especially in startups. Systematics want to build systems for product development, marketing, sales, human resources, finance and accounting, weekly team meetings, board meetings, status meetings, and the list will go on and on. Too many systematics will slow down everything.

Teams need the right people in the right seats. If people are in the wrong places, you are going to have a bad time. Why do people create disorder in a system they are paid to organize or at least maintain? The answer is the person is not in the right role. When people are in positions for which they are unprepared, they will become net creators of disorder.

Missing Knowledge

When anyone is in a role without the required knowledge, the result is incompetence and disorder. It has been said that it is easier to trust malicious people than incompetent people. You can usually predict what malicious people will do, while the incompetents can cause more harm.

Incompetents don't have the essential knowledge or the experience that teaches them about the results of their decisions. They don't have the capacity, or the raw talent, to be able to accomplish their assigned tasks.

Missing Motivation

When team members are malicious, it means they intend to create disorder voluntarily and purposefully. The intention can be to disrupt operations through hacking and deleting information or it can be to steal money and enrich themselves through fraud.

Annually in the United States, blue-collar crime costs $14 billion, and white-collar crime costs $200 billion. Each year in the United States white collar criminals steal an amount equal to two times the IPO value of Facebook.

Bernie Madoff was highly competent, knowledgeable and respected in investment circles in New York City. Madoff also stole $20 billion and said, "I cannot offer you an excuse for my behavior. How do you excuse betraying thousands of investors who entrusted me with their life savings?"

Creative as a Systematic

Creatives can't be systematics. Creatives make systems that expect bureaucrats to figure out everything on their own. Creatives prefer to use their expertise and their imagination to solve problems and expect others to do the same. Creatives can articulate well what the result should look like and generate great ideas on what could be, but the result is always more disorganization.

Systematic as a Creative

When systematics are in a creative role, the result is a stifling environment that will grind creativity. Systematics want to control the creative process by instituting stringent process. If systematics are working with creatives, expect the creatives to become significantly frustrated or to leave the team.

Bureaucrat as a Creative or Systematic

A bureaucrat just wants to follow the rules, so when a bureaucrat attempts creative or systematic work, there is no inspiration. Bureaucrats can do anything you want them to do; they just can't figure out on their own what they should be doing. Bureaucrats feel an immense amount of anxiety at the ambiguity of creative and systemic work. Creatives thrive in ambiguity and systematics shine in chaos, but the lack of structure cripples bureaucrats.

Creative as a Bureaucrat

Having a creative in a bureaucrat role is torture for everyone on the team. Creatives can see opportunities all around them, but they have no authority to make changes. Creatives can't follow the rules because they don't think they apply to them. Creatives can see the meaning behind the rules and are comfortable in complying with the intent of the rules, but they don't want to be constrained by what they see as arbitrariness of the exact specifications.

Systematic as a Bureaucrat

There is a designed process that the systematic enjoys, but the problem is that over time the systematic will feel the frustration of not being able to improve the system. The systematic will have no freedom over the work and the process, and eventually, this begins to wear down the systematic.

Team Size

Sam Altman, the president of Y Combinator, the world's most successful startup incubator, wrote that his advice is to move fast and stay focused. "I have never, not once, seen a slow-moving founder be successful… Companies building rockets and nuclear reactors still manage to do this. All failing companies have a pet explanation for why they are different and don't have to move fast."[71] A balanced team continues to change, stays focused, and moves as fast as it is able.

Team size is the most important factor in moving fast. The ideal size is more than one and a maximum of seven. Ideally, team size should be two to five. David Graeber is an anthropologist at London School of Economics; he was able to capture the problem with large groups and bureaucracy in his book *The Utopia of Rules: On Technology, Stupidity, and the Secret Joys of Bureaucracy*:

> *I think our collective fascination with the mythic origin of Silicon Valley and the Internet have blinded us to what's going on. It has allowed us to imagine that research and development is now driven, primarily, by small teams of plucky entrepreneurs, or the sort of decentralized cooperation that creates open-source software. It isn't. These are just the sort of research teams most likely to produce results. If anything, research has been moving in the opposite direction. It is still driven by giant, bureaucratic projects; what has changed is the bureaucratic culture. The increasing interpenetration of government, university, and private firms has left all parties to adopt language, sensibilities, and organizational forms that originated in the corporate world. While this might have helped somewhat in speeding up the creation of immediately marketable products—as this is what corporate bureaucracies are designed to do—in terms of fostering original research, the results have been catastrophic.*[72]

There are many disadvantages to large teams, but I want to focus on those that affect speed. Jeff Bezos, Amazon's leader, uses the idea of a "two pizza box team." He reasons that if you can't feed a team with two pizzas, it's too large. When some managers at an offsite retreat suggested that Amazon employees should communicate more with each other, Mr. Bezos stood up and declared, "No, communication is terrible!"[73]

The reason that communication is terrible is that it slows down the team's collaboration. The team is a network of individuals who have to communicate with other members of the team. Metcalfe's Law shows that the number of connections within a group increases as the team grows. The principle is illustrated below. Three people can make only three connections, five can make ten connections, and fourteen can make ninety-one connections.

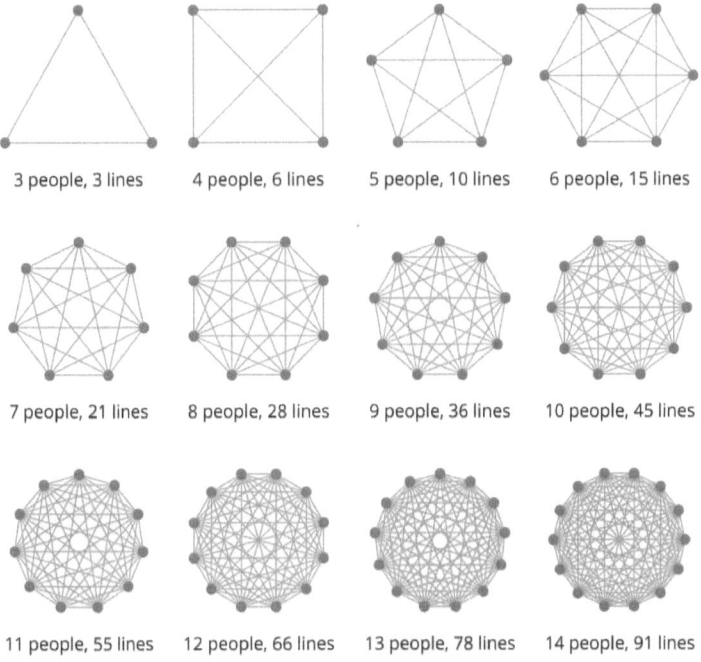

As Marc Andreessen has written, a large team "slows everything in your company to a crawl because there are simply too many people running around who have to talk about everything before anything gets done."[74]

When a team is first formed, each new member helps the team accomplish more, and the team becomes more efficient. However, any team reaches a point when adding one more member does not help.

Eventually adding more members will cause a decrease in the productivity of the entire team.

What happens in practice is that not each person communicates with everyone else, but pockets of communication develop in which a member interacts with some but not all others on the team. For any conversation to spread, it must spread from group to group, which is much slower and less accurate. The team must stop producing and begin communicating about producing.

The Gang Analyzes Mismatched Roles

Markus: Outsourced Development

Give me an example of a time you were in a mismatched role.

> *I worked for a year as an executive assistant for a family friend in his small business. I needed to find a job, and they needed help. I messed everything up.*

Do you have the right team for your idea?

> *I need a creative I trust to manage software development, and I need a systematic to help with sales and to create and document the standard operating procedures.*

Sarah: Interviewing Service

Give me an example of a time you were in a mismatched role.

> *I am a systematic. I like creating order and systems and improving critical processes. When I first started my career in the family company, I started in sales, where I didn't have any power to change or improve anything. I had to work for a manager who was good at doing what he was told but didn't have a vision or ambition to improve things. There was a lot I had to learn about the products we sold and sales techniques, but it was torture working a sales process that I knew I could improve.*

Do you have the right team for your idea?

> *I am not sure that I have the right creative team. They are profoundly influential in the beginning, but I don't want to give them tons of equity to help launch something when I don't need*

them on an ongoing basis. Also, I will need to recruit someone to make our interview assessments.

Joko: Audio Algorithm

Give me an example of a time you were in a mismatched role.

In my first job out of college I was working through updating and maintaining legacy code and 90 percent of my time was spent fixing bugs and not developing new features. This also meant a lot of time on documentation. I hated it, and I learned nothing new. Eventually, I was moved to work on other projects. If I had stayed on those first projects for much longer, I would have quit.

Do you have the right team for your idea?

I thought that I just needed a designer to make things look good and a sales guy to go out and sell. But, to focus on the technology, I need to raise some money and hire creatives with the expertise to take the software to the next level.

PART 5: ORGANIZATIONAL STRUCTURES

Popular real estate advice is that the three most important things about property are location, location, location. The place where you decide to start, grow, and maintain innovation influences the projects you can select and the resources you have available.

If you had nearly unlimited resources to allocate on developing innovation, how would you structure your spending? Alphabet, Google's parent company, doesn't have unlimited resources, but it does have an annual gross margin of $62 billion. Over the next ten years, Alphabet will have $620 billion to spend on promoting innovation.

"Structure follows strategy" is a phrase coined in 1962 by Alfred DuPont Chandler Jr., a professor at Harvard Business School. It is meant to convey that corporate structure is created to implement a given strategy.[75] Successfully developing an innovation is dependent on the structure where the innovation originates, grows, and is maintained. Alphabet uses a combination of structures to achieve its strategic imperative of continuous innovation. This imperative is noted in the Founders' IPO Letter that Google's Larry Page and Sergey Brin wrote in 2004 and titled *"An Owner's Manual" for Google's Shareholders*:

> *We will not shy away from high-risk, high-reward projects because of short term earnings pressure. Some of our past bets have gone extraordinarily well, and others have not. Because we recognize the pursuit of such projects as the key to our long-term success, we will continue to seek them out. For example, we would fund projects that have a 10% chance of earning a billion dollars over the long term. Do not be surprised if we place smaller bets in areas that seem very speculative or even strange when compared to our current businesses. Although we*

cannot quantify the specific level of risk we will undertake, as the ratio of reward to risk increases, we will accept projects further outside our current businesses, especially when the initial investment is small relative to the level of investment in our current businesses.[76]

The various structures that Alphabet chooses are designed to accomplish a specific objective based on what type and grade of innovation they are attempting to achieve. Alphabet engages in the following structures:

- Sustaining operations, such as improved efficiency in data centers.
- New product development aligned with its core businesses, which have resulted in Gmail and AdSense.
- Joint ventures to acquire a specialty that it doesn't have in-house, such as working with automobile manufacturers to develop self-driving cars.
- Research in several technological domains. Pushing the boundaries of the entire ecosystem by publishing proprietary research, research grants, and open challenges.
- Innovation lab, now called X, to explore "moonshot" innovations.
- GV, formerly Google Ventures, which invests in companies outside of the conglomerate.
- Acquisition of businesses and projects, such as its purchase of YouTube.

Sustaining Operations

The top four websites worldwide based on traffic are Google, Facebook, YouTube, and Gmail. Google, YouTube, and Gmail are all Alphabet products. Managing all the traffic and data from those sites requires a tremendous amount of networking, data management, distributed systems and parallel computing, server hardware and architecture, security, privacy, and energy consumption.

Google standardizes its data centers to reduce waste and costs. It has implemented standard procedures to cut costs, complexities, and increase security.[77] There are security teams, privacy teams, internal audits, and compliance specialists. Internal processes are so tight that recently a data center passed an incredible milestone: 3 million working hours with zero lost time incidents. [78]

While operations seek organizational stability, developers seek change and testers want risk reduction.[79] To manage these opposing forces, Google engages in dev-ops, an approach in which building, testing, and releasing software can happen rapidly, frequently, and more reliably.[80] The speed and scale at Google is hard to conceive. More than five thousand developers in forty offices are working on more than two thousand active projects and running more than 100 million test cases a day. Making a significant investment in the central tools team results in a measurable boost in engineer productivity, saving six hundred person-years from 2008-2009.[81]

New Product Development

Alphabet innovates by improving its core and ancillary products and services. It does this through structured and unstructured projects. In the 2004 Founders' IPO Letter the founders claim that this is a strategic decision and that the organization naturally supports these kinds of initiatives.

> *...we expect to devote the vast majority of our resources to improvements to our main businesses (currently search and advertising). Most employees naturally gravitate toward incremental improvements in core areas, so this tends to happen naturally.[82]*

Gmail was launched April 1, 2004. Larry Page, Google co-founder, claimed that the origin of Gmail came from user frustration with other email services at the time, such as Hotmail and Yahoo Mail.[83] It was a structured project, or in other words an executive decision to build a new email service. Paul Buchheit, Gmail's creator, stated: "It was an official charge, I was supposed to build an email thing."[84]

Development of Gmail took over two years, and internal disagreement arose on whether email should be a focus. Buchheit said: "A lot of people thought it was a very bad idea, from both a product and a strategic standpoint. The concern was this didn't have anything to do with web search. Some were also concerned that this would cause other companies such as Microsoft to kill us. Larry [Page] and Sergey [Brin] were always supportive."

The email service was, in the end, closely related to Google's core business of search and advertising. The foundation of Gmail was use of Google technology to search emails, and the revenue model was display of text advertisements based on the content of emails.

To leverage the power of search and provide more and better ads, Gmail needed to motivate users to save a greater number of emails. Google elected to allow a 1GB storage limit, 500 times larger than the industry standard storage limits. As of February 1, 2016, Gmail had over 1 billion users.

Some of Alphabet's products come from employees taking the initiative to work on a project in their spare time. In fact, Alphabet encourages employees, in addition to their regular projects, to spend 20 percent of their time working on unstructured projects they think will benefit the company. This time encourages employees to be more creative and innovative. The 2004 Founders' IPO Letter laid out the 20 percent allotment:

> *Many of our significant advances have happened in this manner. For example, AdSense for content and Google News were both prototyped in "20% time." Most risky projects fizzle, often teaching us something. Others succeed and become attractive businesses.*

AdSense allows websites and blogs to monetize their sites by delivering Google ads alongside their content. Google uses its web-search technology to scan the site content (and other relevant factors) to determine which ads to deliver.

AdSense (Google Network Members' websites) for the fiscal year ending December 31, 2015, generated $15 billion, or 20 percent of total revenue.[85]

Research

Google benefits from fast moving technology and a constantly changing industry because it is positioned to move quickly and incorporate these changes through products/services and operations. Google Research is intended to drive innovation throughout the entire ecosystem and maintain Google at the forefront of the change.

Google conducts research in several of the most challenging technological domains. It (selectively) publishes findings to engage others outside of the company. Google Research has produced 21 research areas (computer science and related fields), 3,552 published articles often tested through real product implementation at scale, 19 public research datasets, and 20 million lines of code on 900 open source code projects

Google Research does outreach to support academic research by providing funding, open tools, data, and code. Here are three representative grant programs;

Faculty Research Awards. One year grants to support the cost of one graduate student in one of eighteen domain areas.[86]

Focused Research Awards. Multi-year projects granted on an invite-only basis to support research in one of the twenty-one domains.[87]

Google Earth Engine Research Awards. One year gifts of up to $150,000 to support research in the area of geospatial data analysis.[88]

Google Research also promotes open challenges to solve pressing problems. For example, in February 2016 Google and IEEE awarded a $1 million prize for creating a smaller energy inverter.[89] Inverters are the boxes that take direct current from a device like solar panels and turn it into alternating current to be used by other electrical equipment. The challenge rewarded the team that could fit an inverter into the smallest rectangular enclosure while maintaining minimum specifications.[90] Teams retained their intellectual property, but published technical approach documents. Electrical engineering experienced a breakthrough and Google may use "these improvements (to) make our data centers run more safely and efficiently."

Joint Ventures

Joint ventures are another way for Alphabet to engage innovation by focusing on its specialization but spanning technical disciplines through another organization. A joint venture is an arrangement in which two or more parties agree to pool their resources for a new project. Joint ventures often include a licensing agreement by the parties that define the compensation and regulate the use of the proprietary information.[91]

Through the innovation lab, X, Alphabet used its expertise in miniaturized electronics, low power chip design, and microfabrication to develop smart contact lenses. But it needed to acquire expertise in physiology and visual performance of the eye, clinical development, FDA approval and other aspects of evaluation, as well as commercialization of contact and implant lenses. To that end, Alphabet entered into a license agreement with Novartis, a multinational pharmaceutical company with $50 billion in annual revenue.

Novartis is focused on two areas: Continuous measurement of tear fluid to monitor glucose levels in diabetic patients (the lens sends the readings wirelessly to a mobile device); and providing autofocus correction on near objects for people living with presbyopia (farsightedness), who can no longer read without glasses.

Innovation Labs

Some types of projects benefit by being separate from ongoing operations. A reason to separate these projects could include an increased need for secrecy and limiting the number of people can accomplish that. It could be to increase work speed by sidestepping quality assurance during development or by the suspension of procurement restrictions. It could also be to explore new products or services outside of the core business. This structure was made famous by Lockheed Martin's Skunk Works.

The launch of the Skunk Works division occurred during World War II. In 1943 the United States needed to respond to Germany's development and deployment of jet fighters. Lockheed's chief engineer, Clarence "Kelly" Johnson, received a secretive project with a very tight deadline. Johnson promised the Pentagon a jet fighter prototype in 150 days. He selected a group of engineers and separated them from the rest of the factory. His engineers developed a prototype in 143 days, creating the P-80 Shooting Star.

Since 1943 Skunk Works has pursued the mission to "build the world's most experimental aircraft and breakthrough technologies in abject secrecy at a pace impossible to rival." It has won six Collier trophies, the most prestigious award in the aeronautics industry. The speed and approach were recorded in Kelly Johnson's logbook while working to prepare the U-2 for its first test flight on July 15, 1955. "Airplane essentially completed. Terrifically long hours. Everybody almost dead."[92]

Alphabet has an innovation lab, now called X, to pursue "moonshots." Since 2010, X has been led by Astro Teller, an entrepreneur, and scientist. Teller holds a bachelor of science degree in computer science, a master of science degree in symbolic computation from Stanford University, and a doctorate in artificial intelligence from Carnegie Mellon University. X's projects have included the self-driving car, Google Glass and Google Lens, Project Loon (delivering the Internet via balloons), Makani (kites that generate energy), and a drone delivery service dubbed Project Wing.

In an annual report filed with the Securities and Exchange Commission, Alphabet claims:

> *Many companies get comfortable doing what they have always done, making only incremental changes. This incrementalism leads to irrelevance over time, especially in technology, where change tends to be revolutionary, not evolutionary.*[93]

X aims for revolutionary change, what it calls moonshots. In February 2016 Teller defined what X looks for and his definition of moonshots, in an open blog post:

> *We look for a huge problem in the world that affects many millions of people. Then we try to propose a radical solution for solving that huge problem. And third, there needs to be some reason to believe that the technology for such a radical solution could actually be built. Some glimmer of hope to get us going and some clear first few steps we could take along that*

205

> *journey... We spend most of our time breaking things and working to discover that we're wrong. That's it. That's the secret. Run at all the hardest parts of a problem first. Ask cheerfully, "How are we going to try to kill our project today!"*[94]

Serious problems that have not been solved are either very difficult or impossible. Teller and his X team want to figure that out as quickly as possible. Once a breakthrough is made, the project graduates out of X.

Venture Fund

Alphabet allocates $400 million a year to fund companies outside of its conglomerate through the GV venture fund (formerly called Google Ventures). GV is a venture capital firm, with a total of $2.4 billion under management, which invests money in startups and also provides specialty support in life science, design, engineering, recruiting, and marketing.[95]

Larry Page, Alphabet's CEO, has told Bill Maris, CEO of GV, "Do as much as you can, as fast as you can in as big and disruptive a way as possible," and even inquired "What do you think you could do with a billion a year?"[96] [97]

The tactical purpose, like any other venture fund, is to earn a financial return. The venture capital model is needed for three reasons. First, it recognizes Alphabet does not hold a monopoly on good ideas. Second, being a startup outside of the conglomerate can provide greater flexibility and responsiveness to the market and improve execution. Finally, it allows startups to compete directly against any other Alphabet company and receive financial benefits if a startup that GV has backed is sold to an Alphabet competitor.[98][99]

Acquisition and Integration

Alphabet acquires companies or projects when they complement its business, and if the project is something Alphabet cannot build itself, such as YouTube.[100]

YouTube has been a part of Google since 2006 and feels like a homemade Google product. Indeed, the product has grown alongside Google. YouTube only spent a little more than a year as a standalone company, and it was Google's largest acquisition at the time.

Google didn't purchase YouTube to make up for a failure to foresee the trend in online videos. It didn't buy YouTube because the technology was too complicated. It didn't purchase YouTube because YouTube had a specialty that Google didn't have.

Susan Wojcicki is the current CEO of YouTube and employee number 16 of Google. She played a critical role in the $1.65 billion purchase of the video-sharing website. In 2006 Wojcicki was running a department called Google Video that was losing to a plucky startup. The startup, YouTube, was not generating revenue and had significant copyright concerns.

"I knew it was going to be really hard for us to catch up, and that this was a real phenomenon," Wojcicki said. "I understood it, because we had our own product." In just one day Wojcicki developed a financial model and presented it to Google's board of directors who approved the acquisition.[101]

In the 2015 annual financial report, Alphabet stated: "People thought we were crazy when we acquired YouTube… But [YouTube has] matured into major platforms for digital video."[102]

There is no one correct answer to how to create, cultivate, and sustain innovation. Alphabet's various structures are a great reminder that each structure is designed based on what type and grade of innovation you are attempting to accomplish. "Structure follows strategy," and there is no one correct answer to strategy.

The Gang Analyzes Innovation Structure

What structure is best for your idea?

Markus: Outsourced development

> *Working inside a corporation could be possible, but I think all the creatives would eventually get bored working on the same types of projects. A startup company is perfect for my idea.*

Sarah: Interviewing Service

> *I think a startup is the best place for the idea. It could be a feature for a recruiting company, but it wouldn't have the legs to be able to grow to job-seekers working with other recruiters.*

Joko: Audio Algorithm

I think in a startup we would have the flexibility to go wherever the technology takes us. But, in a larger company we would have more resources and could focus on the technology and not some of the business aspects, such as running the company and raising money. I think a startup is the best place, but if Google or Apple wanted to support us and give us autonomy, I would say yes.

PART 6: DIFFUSION PROCESS

Product/market fit means being in a good market with a product that can satisfy that market. This section describes how to navigate the four phases of product/market fit.

Customers come in four types, not one, and each is characterized by the diffusion-of-innovation curve: innovators, early adopters, early majority, and late majority. Laggards are so late in the innovation process they are not potential customers and only useful to understand non-adoption. Each type of customer is influenced to accept innovation for very different reasons, and they do not make decisions independent of their social groups, they make decisions in tandem with group decisions. These social groups drive the product/market fit phases and influence whether a client adopts the technology.

To be successful in spreading your innovation, you need to understand how groups are structured to help them consider and accept the technology. Every social group creates norms, which are expectations of behavior that everyone designates as normal and desirable. The social group accepts the rules as valuable to promote group welfare. Your innovation needs to be consistent with those norms. Social groups create a structure to bestow status to individuals who improve the lives of other members. Your technology cannot decrease the status of individual members; ideally, it should increase status. Of course, people in the group gossip about how well others comply with the norms and promote the group welfare. You need to leverage gossip to help the social group talk about your innovation.

Adopters

In conditions of uncertainty, humans, like other animals, herd together for protection.
—James Surowiecki, *The Wisdom of Crowds*

Innovation spreads one user at a time, but groups of users are profiled and segmented based on their timing and reasons for adoption: innovators, early adopters, early and late majority, and laggards. These groups are not statistical classifications. More importantly, the groups describe the adoption process.

Everett Rogers, an author and professor, published his book *Diffusion of Innovations* in 1962 to explain how and why new ideas and technology spread. Diffusion of innovation is when the knowledge of the innovation is spread so that it can be properly understood and potential customers can make an informed decision to adopt or reject the innovation. The chart below shows the types of adopter with the adoption curve of a new technology in black and its market share in grey. In mathematics, the gray curve is known as the logistic function, and here it shows the cumulative market share of the innovation.

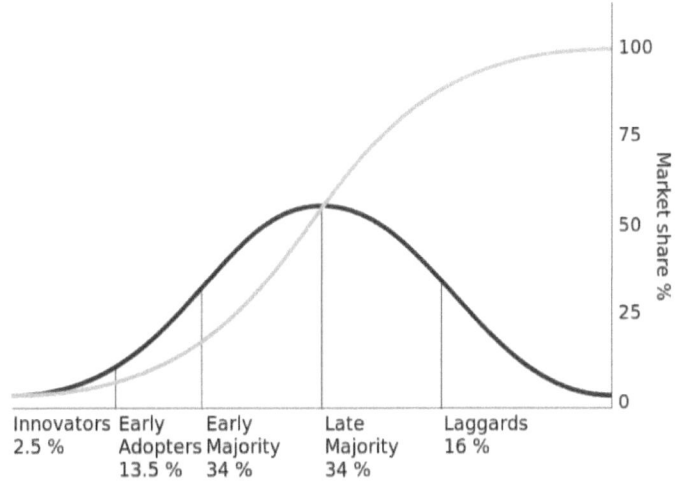

The phases defined by Rogers are not just parts of the adoption process. They are social groups that you need to navigate individually. It is essential to know for whom you are building a product and how to engage with their social group.

Innovators

Innovators are attracted to the novelty of technology. They are technophiles, people who love technology. Innovators want to see the technological boundaries pushed and will purchase each new gadget, subscribe to new services, and will keep updated on the progress of developing technology. Innovators care less about what the technology can accomplish than how the technology is created and how well it does what it claims.

As the grade of innovation is more speculative more innovators are attracted to the technology. Technology is more attractive if it is more difficult to accomplish because it breaks previous constraints. If a new technology claims a 10x improvement, then innovators want to verify those claims and understand the underlying technology.

There are six innovation grades starting with AAA, the lowest risk, and ending with D, the highest risk. Each level has an inverse relationship in the quality of the innovation and the risks of the innovation. This means the innovation with the largest impact is Grade D, a speculative grade, because it also carries the most risk.

At each grade innovators show the following level of interest and want answers to the following questions. You should be prepared to answer them.

Rating-Grade	Type	Interest	Innovator Questions
AAA	Trailing Industry Standards	None	N/A
AA	Industry Standards	Little	How do you compare to other alternatives?
A	Leading Industry Standards	Medium	Where are you leading the industry?
B	Mimetic	High	Can you transition effectively to the new industry?
C	Wave	Curious	Have you identified an opportunity others don't see?
D	Decade	Very High	Can you create a 10x improvement with no close substitute?

If you want to attract innovators, focus your communication on the technology and the improvements over the prior versions or other options available in the industry. The communication can be technical because the details are how an innovator distinguishes the advancement of the technology. The risk of communicating technical specifications is that other groups will hear the message. None of the other groups care about the specs like innovators.

Early Adopters

Early adopters want the product to solve a problem. Early adopters don't care about the underlying technology like innovators, but they do care what the technology can do for them. The grades of innovation are important because they communicate how much of an improvement the product will make for the problem they are trying to solve.

If you want to attract early adopters, focus on the problems that the technology is solving. Use the product motivations to communicate with early adopters: consumption, investment, saving, insurance.

The first approach to scarcity is to use a resource to accomplish a useful activity. The reason why customers are looking to consume is binary: the customer is consuming the product either to relieve some pain or to gain some level of pleasure. There are many different ways people refer to this: wants vs. needs, business vs. pleasure, vitamins vs. painkillers.

Investment is the desire to leverage a resource with the expectation that the usefulness will repay more than the original cost.

Saving means using a scarce resource to avoid or reduce the spending of other resources. A buyer is looking to spend resources that will save money, time, talents, use of machines, or other resources.

Many people are familiar with the concept of insurance through buying policies that protect against the risk of loss.

Early Majority

The transition from early adopter to early majority is difficult, because adoption is no longer about the product. Early majority is the group of adopters that relies primarily on social systems. If other people are not using the product, then the early majority will not. The early majority waits for signals from early adopters to demonstrate value of the innovation. Early majority members care about the innovation because they see others care about it. Of course product performance is important, and the members of this group have a problem to be solved. But the product and the problem are only the foundations, not the reasons for adoption.

If you want to communicate well with the early majority then you highlight social proof using your product, identify an authority figure in their social group who can endorse the product, and help people they like to adopt the product. These weapons of influence will facilitate adoption.

Late Majority

The late majority likes to wait until the market has settled on two or three technological alternatives. The late majority is part of a social system that reduces uncertainty by waiting for the signal from the industry that is has accepted the product. Late majority members wait until the selections are limited and consolidated.

Like with the early majority, of course, product performance is essential, and the members of this group have a problem to be solved. Again, the product and the problem are only the foundations, not the reasons for adoption. Products that become market leaders tell the late majority that those are the best products that solve the problem in the best way possible.

If you want to communicate with the late majority, then you need to know that the industry options are already consolidating around a few market leaders. You need to focus on teaching what attributes make you the top choice in the industry. It is best if you can identify an authority figure in the group who can vouch for market position, such as through published rankings or awards. Late majority members believe that all they need to know is communicated to them by the market leaders.

The Gang Analyzes Adopters

Markus: Outsourced Development

Who are your innovators?

> *Some clients want to push the boundaries of technology and explore what is possible. I have seen it with "big data" and now with "machine learning." Many people want to explore what is possible. These clients are a lot of fun to work with because their projects are more open and more undefined.*

Who are your early adopters?

> *Other clients need to use software to solve a business problem. These are the early adopters. But fortunately for business, in this industry, there are a lot of early majorities that see other companies developing software, and they all want to imitate them.*

Sarah: Interviewing Service

Who are your innovators?

I am not sure. I am not doing anything particularly difficult technically.

Who are your early adopters?

Those that need to improve their interview skills the most are those that are professionals, but where there is still significant competition and where their professional networks and track records are not entirely developed. For example, college graduates with less than five years work experience need to be able to take advantage any time they can secure an interview. I think it would be best for me to focus on the major metropolitan areas, where there are a lot of candidates and always a lot of open positions.

Joko: Audio Algorithm

Who are your innovators?

Our innovators are those that like the technology and find what we are working on is really cool. I have a lot of friends that love to play around with the algorithm and see what they can do with it. One friend recorded the presidential debate between Trump and Clinton. I thought the results were interesting.

Who are your early adopters?

The software solves a problem for students and it does better than anything else that I am aware of. Students love it and need it.

Non-Adopters

But many that are first shall be last, and the last shall be first.
–Matthew 19:30

Most innovators focus on the characteristics of early adopters to understand how to generate user adoption. Starting with early adopters is reasonable because by definition early adopters are the first to accept a new technology. Without your first adopters, there are no adopters.

The more insightful analysis is to begin with groups of people that do not and will not adopt innovation and technology. You will benefit more from a careful study of a group of people who consistently reject change because your problem is the potential customers who reject your innovation. To solve that problem, you need to understand why they resist it.

The Amish are traditionalist Christians who reject all recent technological advances. Amish do not use the automobile, radio, television, computers, or the Internet. To be fair, over the centuries the Amish have accepted some technologies, such as indoor flush toilets, running water for bath tubs, propane gas, and tractors. Once you understand why the Amish reject recent innovation, you will have greater insights about all non-adoption of technology. Ultimately this understanding will improve your ability to maneuver all aspects of the diffusion process.

The Amish reject technology because of their social systems. Diffusion is elusive because it spreads one user at a time, but each user is a member of social systems that influence their decisions. The Amish social system is made up of four essential components that affect innovation diffusion. These same social system dynamics affect every industry and every market in every country; they are social norms, structure, gossip, and influencers. Amish social norms, such as their faith tradition and cultural values, influence the way individuals view technology. The second component is the Amish social structure and the way they have organized their society to influence personal decisions. The third comes from the fact that the Amish live and work in small communities, so their communication network is very homogenous. Finally, opinion leaders in the Amish community reinforce the existing social norms and do not deviate from their centurial practices.

There are more than 250,000 Amish in the United States, but there is a sense of public fascination with them because 20 million tourists visit Amish communities each year. Some Amish images are well known: the horse and buggy, the Pennsylvania landscape, the plain clothes, rejection of technological advances, and community barn raising.

Today Amish are found only in the United States and Canada, but the religion began in Europe. To fully understand their current social systems, we need to go back to the beginning, which coincided with the Protestant Reformation in Germany and Martin Luther posting his Ninety-five Theses of 1517. The Amish predecessors were the Anabaptists, who believed that baptism should be done as an adult, and not as an infant as was widely practiced at the time. Anabaptists taught that baptism represents making a commitment and joining a church, which one can only do voluntarily. This view of baptism in the sixteenth century was a combination of heresy and treason and was designated a capital offense. Governments appointed Anabaptist hunters to chase down between two thousand and three thousand adherents and those who survived did so only by hiding.

By the early eighteenth century, a group led by Jakob Ammann left the Anabaptists and started his group called the Amish. The assembly left Switzerland and immigrated to Pennsylvania. They kept a tight community and even continued speaking their native language, now a dialect referred to as Pennsylvania German.

Our next step will be to deconstruct the Amish social system that has rejected innovation for centuries so you can understand how to navigate the social systems you need to spread your technology.

The Gang Analyzes Non-Adopters

Who are your industry non-adopters?

Markus: Outsourced Development

Some organizations are not incorporating custom software into their business and will never need us.

Sarah: Interviewing Service

I think blue-collar or minimum wage workers are my industry non-adopters.

Joko: Audio Algorithm

Who would never adopt the technology? I think we are close to an inflection point where AI and neural lace will redefine what it means to be human and many people will begin to reject technology to live a more traditional human life. In other words, I think humans will integrate computers and computers will become more humanlike and the line will become blurry where one starts and another end. I can see a lot of people just wanting to live a traditional human life.

Social Systems

> *Once mimetic desire starts to snowball, you can get entire communities full of rivalry and strife.*
> —René Girard

When we interact as a group, we create social systems. We naturally form social groups with others who have common interests. In the social group, we promote the interests and goals of the collective, because they are our interests that we believe we can accomplish working together. When there is a new interest to consider, the group will collectively decide if the new thing is good or bad for the group. Social networks are critical to innovation because entire groups send signals to all of the individuals reinforcing why they should or should not adopt technologies.

You are best served by planning any diffusion to occur based on the behavior of the group. It may be possible to stand alone and to make decisions about innovation adoption independently of the group, but it is so rare you should consider it impossible. In Aristotle's book *Politics,* he wrote, "Man is by nature a social animal; an individual who is unsocial naturally and not accidentally is either beneath our notice or more than human. Society is something that precedes the individual. Anyone who either cannot lead the common life or is so self-sufficient as not to need to, and therefore does not partake of society, is either a beast or a god."[103]

The more similar the individuals in a group, the stronger the cohesion will be. This tendency is called homophily. Heterophily is the opposite, where the relationships are relatively weaker and more difficult to maintain.

It's hard to recognize the influence your personal social systems have on you because they are a part of who you are, much like culture.

Normal Behavior

Robert Cialdini, whom some call the "Godzilla" of persuasion, defined social norms as "cultural values, customs, and traditions which represent individuals' basic knowledge of what others do and think that they should do." Social norms define what normal behavior should be to advance the interests of the group. If the group rejects technology, then the group as a whole rejects it.[104]

The Amish have maintained a distrust of the government and general population because of their history and their religious beliefs. The Amish want to live Christ's teachings, and they don't believe that they can continue to live the purity of the doctrine if they integrated with the general population, which does not adhere to the teachings. The Amish believe that many things found in this world are a distraction to spirituality and their relationship with Deity. One Amish adherent stated in a documentary, "The closest you can get to God is working the soil." All of the Amish system norms center on how to be closer to God, and technology is a distraction.

The Amish culture is incompatible with modern culture and use of technology. Amish churches forbid individuals to pose for face-on photos for two reasons. First, they believe it violates the second of the Bible's Ten Commandments: "Thou shalt not make... any graven image, or any likeness of anything....". Second, in a cooperative society that values humility, posing for photos is a sign of pride that calls attention to oneself and contradicts the values of self-sacrifice and group unity.

Use of technology, however, is not uniform among the forty different churches. Each church chooses what technology will serve its community and rejects what may harm it. They are free to modify technology to fit their cultural values, such as placing steel wheels on tractors, installing battery-powered turn signals on buggies, running refrigerators with propane gas, and using computers programs for bookkeeping. All of them have so far chosen to reject television and the ownership of cars.

Your innovation needs to be consistent with norms.

Structure

Social structure is the way social groups organize themselves to achieve their purpose, maintain norms and behavior, and reinforce social status. The Amish have centered their social structure on their church membership and families.

Holding true to Anabaptist roots, to this day Amish members can only officially accept a baptism and join the church as an adult, they learn the Pennsylvania German dialect, and they endorse the local congregation's beliefs and regulations. The community does not shun people who grow up Amish and later decide not to join the church through baptism because those people have not made baptismal commitments.

You need to understand how groups are structured to help them consider and accept the technology.

Status

Groups grant a higher status, power, and influence to individuals who have made the lives of group members better. People with power yield significant influence over the decision of other members on whether to adopt technological advances because they have the trust and have a record of promoting the interests of the group.

Dacher Keltner is a professor of psychology at University of California, Berkeley, where he directs the Berkeley Social Interaction Lab. He wrote a book about power called *The Power Paradox* wherein he defined how social groups grant power. "We gain power by acting in ways that improve the lives of other people in our social networks. Our power is granted to us by others. This is true at work, in social organizations of different kinds, and in our friendships, romantic partnerships, and families."[105]

Amish congregations extend calls of service to members to serve in leadership positions. One of the members serves as bishop, one as a deacon, and one as secretary. Over time these leaders imprint their perspective on the congregation in regard to teaching, doctrine, protocol, dress, and routines. Leaders meet regularly with other leaders within the same area and compare needs, problems, and teachings. Members turn to those in leadership positions for advice, counsel, and direction.

Higher status individuals have more personal connections than the average group member, so their opinions will reach more people more quickly. These views will also create an impression that other people have already reached a consensus. In the end, it often doesn't matter whether an opinion leader of the group is qualified to offer an opinion on your technology or whether the conclusion is right or wrong.

Your technology cannot decrease the status of individual members; ideally, it should increase status.

Gossip

Group gossip refers to the interaction between members of a small group of individuals. Dacher Keltner continues in *The Power Paradox*: "Far from being idle, inconsequential, or easily rooted out of social life, gossip is the sophisticated means by which group members spread information that feeds into reputations. Using gossip, a group can track an individual's likelihood of advancing its interests and determine what power each individual has."[106]

Amish congregations meet every other week for the entire Sunday at a member family's farm. Each member family rotates as host so that during a year each member family serves as host. Congregations share tables, chairs, and wagons and move them from farm to farm every other week. In weeks where they don't meet as a group, most Amish will spend Sunday with their family, neighbors, and personal friends both in and outside of their congregation.

When Amish members break their vows of baptism by disobeying religious leaders or church regulations and refuse to confess their error, they may face excommunication. The Amish use shunning to generate group cohesion and to exclude excommunicated members, to motivate them to acknowledge their mistakes and return to the group's values. Shunning typically involves rituals of shaming such as not eating at the same table with ex-members at weddings or other public gatherings.

You need to leverage gossip to help the social group talk about your innovation.

The Gang Analyzes Social Systems

Markus: Outsourced Development

Describe your target social system.

> *I just need to expand on my existing customer base. One social system of my current customer base is software development for construction companies. It is surprising that they do a lot of software development, but most of the software helps them operate and communicate internally, with other providers, and their clients. Software has a high value for them, they can price it into their contracts, and they can't manage any development internally.*

What are the social norms of your targeted social system?

> *All these guys know each other, and all compete for the same contracts, and employees move around from one company to another depending on who wins the big contract and needs the labor. So, they all compete, but they all respect each other. They care about the safety of their employees and their reputation.*

How is the social system structured?

> *In my areas there is a top tier, middle tier, and lower tier.*

How does the social system confer status?

> *Status is given to the bigger and more prestigious projects that they work on. Winning and building a museum with a famous architect confers more status than another apartment complex. But, a larger apartment complex confers more status than a smaller complex.*

How does the social system gossip?

> *There are no secrets inside this group. Employees move around, and they all compete for the same projects, which can take a long time to negotiate and win and sometimes years to build. When we build software for one client, we can almost guarantee that next year we will develop similar software for another customer.*

Sarah: Interviewing Service

Describe your target social system.

My target system is what I see as early adopters. Young professionals with less than five years professional experience in major metro areas.

What are the social norms of your targeted social system?

The young professionals are at a stage where they are building a network, need to change companies to advance their careers, they value collaboration, taking risks, and growing their expertise.

How is the social system structured?

The social systems are organized by technical expertise. Accountants, lawyers, computer hardware, computer software, and salespeople. They are also structured inside the companies and departments.

This point makes me realize that I should focus on a niche domain and geographic area in the beginning. Such as accounting in New York and software developers in San Francisco.

How does the social system confer status?

Young professionals confer status to those that can develop strong technical abilities in their domain and can take advantage of opportunities with projects or positions.

How does the social system gossip?

There is a lot of gossip inside companies about the performance of co-workers. The social groups also communicate through friends, alumni associations, professional groups, and other networking events.

Joko: Audio Algorithm

Describe your target social system.

I want to start with university students because I understand them and I know the software works. I can continue to improve the software for them and for other commercial uses.

What are the social norms of your targeted social system?

University students are optimistic about the future, they value progress and knowledge. They are digital natives and are comfortable using new technology in any aspect of their life. Students also have a strange combination of collaboration and competition.

How is the social system structured?

There are a couple of different structures in student life based on how students interact with each other. There are systems based on academic departments, sororities and fraternities, individual classes, housing, and of course other living arrangements, either in the dorms or off campus.

How does the social system confer status?

Student social systems confer status a little different depending on how or why it is structured. I think primarily those students who are naturally smarter and work hard are respected. I also think students that work on something outside of their coursework have higher status.

How does the social system gossip?

Students gossip all the time on social media, in study groups, and in their extracurricular activities. Student life is fairly well connected, so when something happens it can spread quickly.

Diffusion Process

The culmination of all the hard work and strategy comes together during the diffusion process. The process itself is easy: cultivate a positive association, reduce uncertainty, and motivate an action. If the customer decides to adopt, then the next steps are to implement and reaffirm the decision. Each step in the diffusion process relies on the type of innovation and the social system of the potential customers.

This chapter focuses on the adoption of a product, but the same process is applied to any of the thirteen innovation types.

Everything impacts diffusion.

Cultivate a Positive Association

The first part of the process is exposing the potential customer individually to the innovation. Potential customers still lack a lot of information, so during this stage you want to inspire them to find out more information. Your tools to accomplish this are your brand, your channels, your governance, and the social system gossip. When potential customers discover your innovation, you will create a positive, neutral, or negative association with them. A positive impression is a goal, but a negative one is workable. Neutral is hard because it is forgettable.

The brand physique and brand personality are often the first exposure. Your name, logo, and other information about your physique and your brand will cultivate the first impressions. Remember, the brand physique and personality reflect how the customer feels about herself and how she wants to be perceived by others.

The channel you have selected to communicate with your potential customers and to distribute the product sends a message about how you want to be perceived and what how you will conduct the interaction. If you have chosen an indirect or direct channel, what are the messages you are communicating?

The people in your hierarchy will create a positive/neutral/negative association. If Peter Thiel, Elon Musk, or Bill Clinton is on your board, then you automatically create a connection to their personal brand. The individuals involved in the governance of your organization tell a double-edged story. If your hierarchy is full of young recent college graduates, you associate yourself with youth, but also inexperience. If your hierarchy is full of influential politicians, you associate yourself with power, but also to their political positions.

Are individuals in the social system talking about your innovation? If you want a positive association, you need someone in the social circles who has a favorable impression and who is willing to spread gossip about you and your product.

Reduce Uncertainty

Innovation creates disorder equal to the level of order the innovation creates, a concept we explored earlier, called The Second Law of Innovation. Be careful not to ignore the disorder or dismiss the impact to the adopter. Adopters suffer from the disorder and aren't always confident that they will be able to manage it. Innovation's disorder can be suffocating, but if it can be sufficiently managed, the innovation can be established as a lasting success.

Uncertainty causes people to fear the new product, which slows adoption. You can integrate features that help potential users understand that the disorder is manageable. When potential users can use the product as part of the decision process, they will be more likely to adopt the new product. The ability to use the product before making a decision is called trialability. Let potential users take your product for a test drive. Inherently observable products spread quicker and further because they allow potential users to discover the product and evaluate the performance before making a decision to adopt it. More importantly, observable products also provide evidence that other people in their social group are using the product. If it works for others, then they know it can work for them.

Products compatible with existing processes and technologies will be adopted quicker than those that are not supported or that are difficult to integrate. If users cannot use the new product with existing systems, it reduces the value, sometimes to zero.

How much time and expertise is needed to implement and learn to operate the product? Complexity slows innovation adoption.

The core process is how the organization creates value. Can the customer expect you to deliver the reliable product you promised to customers? How can you help show potential customers that your core process produces predictable results?

There are innovators and opinion leaders inside a group who are interested in promoting the interests of the group. Members of the group turn to them to form an opinion. A positive opinion from innovators in the group will reduce uncertainty of other members. Do you know who the innovators are and what they think about your innovation?

Use the chart below to assess how your efforts are impacting the awareness and uncertainty.

Diffusion Process: Awareness & Uncertainty		
	Positive Association	**Reduce Uncertainty**
1. Product		Describe characteristics.
2. Funding		
3. Info		
4. Brand	What is the brand impression?	
5. Channel	What is the channel message?	
6. Network		
7. Core Process		Is the result predictable?
8. Enabling Process		
9. Economies of Scale		
10. Culture		
11. Governance	Who is involved in governance?	
12. Customer Service		
Social System	What are people saying?	What do innovators think?

Motivating Action

Potential customers eventually weigh the advantages and disadvantages and make a decision to adopt or reject the innovation. The innovation grades help you to understand and communicate the differentiation and performance that customers receive from your product versus other industry options.

The first four grades are "reasoning by analogy" innovations. These grades are Trailing Industry Standards, Industry Standard, Leading Industry Standards, and Mimetic. The other grades are "reasoning by first principles" innovations, Wave and Decade.

When you know the grade you are delivering, you know what risks might prevent adoption. The risks listed below are accumulative, which means, for example, that the risks for Grade AA include the risks of Grade AAA.

Rating-Grade	Type of Innovation	Risks	Guiding Questions
AAA	Trailing Industry Standards	Systemic and Industry	Is now the right time?
AA	Industry Standards	Distribution and AAA risks	Do you have a way not just to create but deliver your product?
A	Leading Industry Standards	Competition and AA risks	Will your market position be defensible 10 and 20 years into the future?
B	Mimetic	Team and A risks	Do you have the right team?
C	Wave	Financial and Technology and B risks	Is it possible to be profitable while providing the solution? Have you identified an opportunity others don't see?
D	Decade	Regulatory and C risks	Can you create a 10x improvement with no close substitute?

    The value of connecting to a network depends on the number of other things already linked. If the network is important to the customer but your network is just beginning then the product has to have value even without the network. As the network grows the value the customer will receive increases. If you already developed a large network then you need to communicate it clearly with the potential customers.

Economies of scale means the more you produce something, the less it costs to produce each thing. If you are still early in the process and working toward economies of scale, then the customer can expect price decreases as your costs per unit decrease. Technophiles value the underlying technology and want to help firms reach economies of scale, so they are willing to pay higher unit prices while the majority of potential customers wait until the price drops. Integrate your price reductions with the corresponding phases of product market fit. Start with the higher prices with innovators, reduce the price for early adopters, another price reduction for the early majority, and again with the late majority.

Information is extremely useful and also a paradox. Keeping it a secret brings power to the holder, but sharing it brings different power to the giver. Do you have powerful information? Make sure potential customers know the data you are leveraging or disseminating because it will motivate the potential customers to adopt the product.

What happens to customers when a company runs out of funding or goes bankrupt? They go without or must switch to an alternative that they already passed over. Recently I wanted to begin using some software that would help me tremendously, but I delayed because it required a time-consuming setup of sensitive financial information. I was unsure if the software startup would continue to be financially viable. I signed up the day they were acquired by a large tech company. Potential customers need to know that management can consistently deliver what is needed to sustain the organization. Effective management optimizes the enabling process that supports the organization.

Members of the early majority need to know who else is using something to motive their adoption. They look for signals from other people as indicators of the value of the innovation. The early majority does not care about the innovation itself, they care that others are interested. If the early majority does not know that other people are using the product they will not adopt.

Implementation

If potential customers choose to adopt, then they implement the product. This could be as easy as an install from the App Store or as difficult as years of custom engineering.

Part of the implementation process is payment. There are no free lunches. Often the exchange is straightforward, but not always. Is the product funded by revenue, subsidized by equity or taxes, or supported by donations?

The way your group sees the world influences what you do during the implementation process, and there should be a culture fit between you and the customer. Culture is the attitudes and behavior characteristics of a social group, and every group has its own. Culture is the way that the group sees the world. Cultures don't need to be identical to make an implementation successful, but they do need to be compatible in their interactions.

Do not dismiss the risks that your customer will lose status inside his social group during implementation. This is one of the reasons that you need to understand how status is gained and lost in those social groups, because they know. They know how your product will impact their status. You have to get outside of your own head and the status you are clawing for yourself and help your customers gain, or at least preserve, their status in their group.

Reaffirmation

Buyer's remorse is real, and the customer must manage all the disorder created by the implementation of the innovation. If this process goes smoothly, then the customer reaffirms the purchase decision, and if the process has not contained the disorder or delivered on the benefits promised, then the customer will regret the decision.

Your customer service is the way to handle the reaffirmation process. Customer support is not something you do; it is the result of everything you do. If you want to influence customers in a particular way, it requires harmony between every type of innovation. Customer service is a blend of all other types of innovation.

The customer should NEVER lose status in the social group due to the implementation of your product. Dropping status inside the group will be a warning signal to every other potential customer to stay away.

Use the chart below to assess how your efforts are impacting decisions and action.

	Diffusion Process: Decision & Action		
	Motivate Action	Implement	Reaffirm
1. Product	What is the product grade?		
2. Funding		Who pays?	
3. Info	Is the info powerful?		
4. Brand			
5. Channel			
6. Network	Is there a network?		
7. Core Process			
8. Enabling Process	Will the company be here tomorrow?		
9. Economies of Scale	Will the price decrease?		
10. Culture		Is there a culture fit?	
11. Governance			
12. Customer Service			Does the customer regret?
Social System	Who else is using?	Will customer lose status?	Did customer lose status?

EPILOGUE

We are defined not be the technologies we create, but the process in which we create them.
—Skunk Works founder Kelly Johnson

You are lying to yourself. Maybe your lies are inconsequential, or maybe they are major.

You have developed a particular way of seeing the world as a result of all your life experiences. These experiences have illuminated your ideas and showed you the best path for your strategy. The problem is, when you are faced with evidence that contradicts your experiences and your decisions, you feel uncomfortable and will want to resolve the conflict. This is called cognitive dissonance. It is painful, so you lie to yourself.

It would be rational to learn from new information and to adjust your beliefs and plans accordingly. Sometimes you do. Most frameworks expect you to be rational when confronted with conflicting information. Lean Startup suggests you use the scientific method to test a theory by talking to customers and then to iterate, or "pivot" based on what you learn from your customers. What that framework does not account for is how psychologically discomforting the process is and how likely you are to deceive yourself throughout the entire process.

Confirmation bias is a powerful way to avoid the discomfort of cognitive dissonance. Confirmation bias is when you want something to be true you will believe that it is true and you find evidence to confirm it. Once you have formed a view, you embrace information that confirms it while ignoring, or rejecting, information that contradicts it.

An important piece of the innovation process is to receive and incorporate feedback into your strategy. Elon Musk provided the following advice to startup founders:

Be focused on something that has high value to someone else. Be rigorous in making that assessment. Natural human tendencies are wishful thinking. What is the difference between really believing your ideals and sticking to them versus pursuing some unrealistic dream that doesn't have merit? Can you tell the difference between those two things?

Why is telling the difference between believing your ideals and pursuing some unrealistic dream so difficult? The answer comes from a famous quote by Richard Feynman, the American theoretical physicist: "The first principle is that you must not fool yourself — and you are the easiest person to fool."

Using my framework, you will have developed a better understanding of your strategy and will be better prepared than most innovators. As you move forward, you will be your biggest stumbling block. It is something we all do. This is why Elon Musk suggests you be very rigorous in assessing whether you are misleading yourself.

Harder to Fool Other People

If Feynman was correct that you are the easiest to fool, then try to fool someone else. Explain what you believe and show them the evidence and see if they come to the same conclusion.

Find a mentor or a respected advisor to try to fool. Many startups leverage advisors who have built a company before or venture capitalists who serve on their boards.

You need someone because you are lying to yourself. Either you believe me, in which case you know I'm right. Or you don't believe me, in which case you just proved I am right.

APPENDIX

Readers, I have collected the gang's responses in one place to make it easier for you to review the innovation dreams of Markus, Sarah, and Joko. As we have moved through the book we have examined their ideas one step at a time and here you can see the ideas consolidated.

These questions help you understand these concepts, but the exercise also can help you assess your own ideas. After I present the gang's responses I also include all the questions compiled. I encourage you to examine your own ideas by answering the questions. Your answers will be the foundation to creating a one page summary of your winning strategy.

Markus

Markus walks in and says "Hi," shakes my hand, and sits down in the chair on my left. Markus graduated from University of California San Diego with a degree in fine art, digital design. He is a product designer at a small startup but also takes on independent work. Markus has a full beard and is wearing an old faded light blue T-shirt with an image of the Marvel X-Men character Nightcrawler, dark blue skinny jeans, and a black pair of cap-toe oxfords without socks.

"I asked each of you to bring your best idea and to be prepared to discuss. Did you select your best and favorite idea? Markus, let's start with you."

Part 1: Defining Innovation

What is your favorite idea?

> *I do a lot of consulting and contract to work as a designer, even though I have a full-time job. I turn away a lot of good business because I just don't have the time. I want to build an outsourced software development business. I want to work with people I like, clients I like, projects I like, and be able to take off when the surfing is good. I know that I can't do it on my own. I hate sales and business development. Most projects need developers. So, even though I need help with and managing the software developers I could build a good company. I know it wouldn't become a huge company, but I am 100 percent sure it could be a good company.*

Do you see a way that reasoning by analogy guided your idea?

> *Definitely. I have a friend that opened up a marketing and advertising agency a few years ago. He has over 100 employees, and he is making a lot of money. He has been able to craft the company culture as he wants. He loves what he does and is very successful. I turn away business every week, and I look at him and know that we could build something even better.*

Markus, have you used first principles in evaluating and planning your idea?

I have never thought about it this way. I think of my idea and the company I want to create as it relates to Maslow's hierarchy of needs. It is a theory of human motivation, represented by a pyramid. On the bottom of the pyramid are the most basic human needs, such as food, shelter, and clothes. As these requirements are fulfilled people want to feel safe, then belonging, self-esteem and self-respect, and eventually they will want to pursue self-actualization.

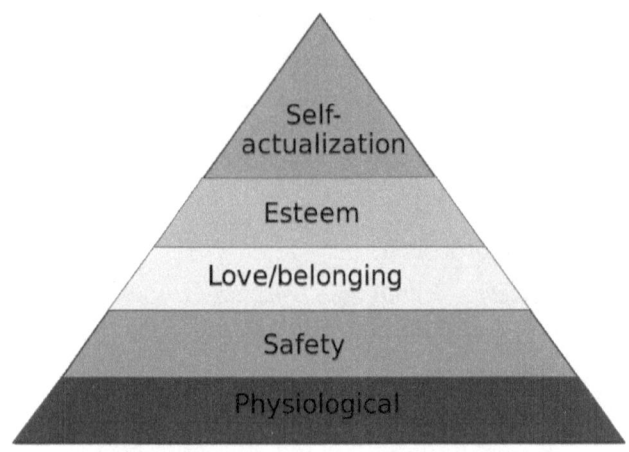

Maslow's Hierarchy of Needs[107]

This idea is critical to my idea and what I want for myself and for the people with whom I work. In fact, building this type of work environment is exciting. I have never worked at a place like that, and I think we could treat people like that and create a fantastic company.

What problem do you want to solve?

Build good software.

What constraints have prevented solving the problem?

There is more demand for skilled designers and developers than there is supply. For companies that develop their software, but where it isn't their primary line of business, it's hard to source and assess the talent of developers and designers.

What is your industry?

Consulting.

What is your "valuable order"?

A pool of shared and vetted professionals.

What do you expect is the most difficult "internal disorder" problem you need to solve?

Managing a consistent culture as we grow.

What do you expect is the most difficult "external disorder" problem you need to solve?

Keeping the brand strong and our interactions with customers.

Part 2: Innovation Grades

Define AAA grade for your industry.

I think Grade AAA for my industry would be what I am doing now. I do one-off projects for clients, on my own with no standard process. I do whatever the client wants. However they want it. The result sometimes is an inconsistent deliverable.

Is now the right time?

Marc Andreessen has said that software is eating the world, meaning that software will disrupt every market. So I believe that software development is and will continue to be an important part of any organization's operations.

Define AA grade for your industry.

Grade AA is small development shops that work with their clients to understand what they need and then contract with foreign developers to implement the design and build the software.

Do you have a way not just to create but deliver your product?

These companies require a robust sales process to be able to identify and close these business opportunities. There is an industry process for this; I think that with this team we could sell a lot.

Define A grade for your industry.

Grade A is the best tech companies. These companies, such as Google and Facebook, are leading software development regarding quality and speed. And for design IDEO is leading the industry. Competition for talent is fierce.

Will your market position be defensible 10 and 20 years into the future?

These leading companies can offer a lot of money, stock options, and career-boosting experience to engineers and designers. Competing with these companies is tough. So, I am not sure how I can compete with them. I might not have a defensible position, but they do.

Define B grade for your industry.

I look at other industries and the way that they operate internally. We can learn from the way law firms are structured with partners and associates. An associate is hired out of law school and has a career pathway from day one. Over time they gain more experience and increase their professional network. They are managed by a partner who is responsible for the book of business and quality control of the services. Each partner is kind of a mini-company inside the firm. Many software firms break out and are small companies, or they are organized around middle managers.

Do you have the right team?

I think I have the right team for where I am right now. But, if I implemented this type of structure, do I have someone who can architecture the structure? No. So, I would need to work with someone who knows very well the compensation structure, duties of the partners and associates, and the skill sets that define each position. Then, I would need to make sure that I maintain the vision so that additional hires are made in the right role and I could help associates progress to become partners.

Is there a group that has historically been underfunded, understaffed, and as a result has gone without? Is this group likely to appreciate lower cost "good enough" solutions?

> *In my industry I think that the way outsourced software development has evolved includes some aspects of Grade C. Software development in the United States has been very expensive and required technical and management skills to be able to create effective software. As a result, many companies did not create customized software for their needs.*

Is it possible to be profitable while providing the solution?

> *Yes, by using developers with very different economic needs. Over the past few years, many consulting companies have partnered with overseas developers to lower the cost of software development. It is easy to be profitable even under the traditional model.*

Have you identified an opportunity others don't see?

> *I don't think I see anything special. Many people are adopting similar models. This discussion is helpful because innovators who can improve and maintain quality will be able to provide services to the whole market.*

Can you create a 10x improvement with no close substitute?

> *I am not sure what kind of innovation would be a 10x improvement. It would mean getting forty hours of software development in four hours, or keeping quality high and paying ten dollars to the one dollar for the costs. Not sure what could cause that to happen.*

Could your idea create or face any new regulations?

> *No.*

Part 3: Innovation Types

Describe buyer motivations for your product and the five product characteristics.

Consumption:

> My clients' intrinsic motivation would be just to have good software. Like, the software just does what it is supposed to do. A customer has a job to do, and the software helps do that job.

Investment:
> My clients' investment motivation is usually to create their product or enhance their existing products to generate more revenue. They spend money on development, and the result is an asset that can return more money to the company.

Saving:
> My clients want to save money by hiring an outsourced development shop because the costs of hiring and managing their full-time staff quickly add up and can be more than the consulting rates. It could also be that the software enables them to save money somewhere else, such as server resources or automating something that requires staff time.

Insurance:
> If my clients hire us, or any other outsourced development company, they may want to insure the risk of trying to manage the development internally. Years ago (when IBM was the gold standard) people used to say "Nobody ever got fired for buying IBM." So, if a project fails, but you hired a consulting firm with a good reputation, then you have someone to blame. If you do it internally and you mess up then you only have yourself to blame.

Negative Value:
> Many of my clients have hired outsourced development shops, spending a lot of money only to have unusable software at the end. So, there is a real risk of spending money on time and not having any usable results. I guess it could even be worse than that because it could be useful software that sucks and has lots of problems.

Describe how you can improve your product based on the five product characteristics:

Relative Advantage:

The relative advantage of our services is measured by the speed and the quality of the services. I think being at industry standard is sufficient.

Compatibility:

I believe that this gets to having developers that know the languages that our clients need. If we can't integrate with their tech or with what their requirements are, then we are not helpful.

Complexity:

We can reduce complexity by making it easier to work with us, from contracts, to project scoping, to updates and iterations.

Trialability:

Having a trialable service is difficult. I think the closest we could get is to have guaranteed or your money back. But, I have done enough design projects to know that it doesn't work in practice. I don't think I could offer a trial period.

Observability:

I usually do this when we have worked on some public projects. We can show the products we have built, and that helps potential clients to see the quality of our work.

Describe how you could use each of the four funding sources.

Equity:

I would use equity to motivate cofounders and other valuable employees. I might have to raise some money from investors to help provide cash to grow.

Revenue:

Essentially we are selling our time, or we are selling a deliverable. Revenue is easy for this business. There are a lot of customers lining up to buy already.

Government:

This one's hard. I think the best I can come up with is the fact that our customers deduct our charges on their taxes. Maybe I would have to talk to a tax accountant to know what tax advantages are available to us. Like hiring military veterans for some roles.

Donations:

Okay, this one's hard too. One idea might be that we could use blogs to help market our services and we might be able to get some guest spots that we could use which would assist the guest author in their career.

Which funding source will you focus on?

I hope that revenue can fund almost everything. I have a good pipeline now, and margins are pretty good, so if we grow purposefully, then I might not need to be in any outside investment. Government and donations don't actually provide any other critical support.

Describe how you could use information dissemination and information accumulation with your product.

This is difficult. I don't think there is any information that we can release back to nature or put in a zoo.

What impression do you want to convey with your brand?

I want to convey creativity and innovation, but with predictable results. That is a tricky combination, but clients want something original but reliable. I want them to have the impression that we can deliver on their projects.

Describe how customers in your industry want your brand to make others perceive them.

Customers want to look smart and talented. Clients are working on important company projects that will impact their careers. So, they want to look like they got the best that the company can buy. It doesn't have to be the most expensive or the highest quality.

Describe what your brand makes customers feel about themselves.

Customers want to build confidence in themselves about their management decisions.

Highlight your brand personalities.

I know this might be weird, but I see two personalities. One for design and another for software development. The left brain is analytical, and the right brain is creative. Our brand has to balance both sides of the brain

For the creative brain:

Personality	High	Low
Conscientiousness	Efficient, Hard-working, Well-organized	**Easy-Going, Negligent, Lazy, Disorganized**
Agreeableness	**Friendly, Trusting, Lenient**	Analytical, Ruthless, Critical
Neuroticism	**Nervous, Emotional, Worried**	Confident, Unemotional, Calm
Openness	**Curious, Creative, Imaginative**	Cautious, Conventional, Down-to-earth
Extraversion	**Outgoing, Talkative, Active**	Reserved, Loner, Quiet

For the analytical brain:

Personality	High	Low
Conscientiousness	**Efficient, Hard-working, Well-organized**	Easy-Going, Negligent, Lazy, Disorganized
Agreeableness	Friendly, Trusting, Lenient	**Analytical, Ruthless, Critical**
Neuroticism	Nervous, Emotional, Worried	**Confident, Unemotional, Calm**
Openness	Curious, Creative, Imaginative	**Cautious, Conventional, Down-to-earth**
Extraversion	Outgoing, Talkative, Active	**Reserved, Loner, Quiet**

What are your industry's standard direct and indirect channels?

The standard is each group hires a sales development team and marketing department to market and sell its services.

What is your direct channel approach?

Our approach is what we have been currently doing, manage sales directly.

Is the sales process documented and can it easily be communicated to sales people?

No. The sales process is very consultative, and clients like to talk to the person that will manage the project (the person who knows what they are talking about). Of course, a salesperson is needed to start the conversation and to close the sale. I hate that whole process, but I love sitting down with clients and learning how I can help them.

Is there an existing demand that partners can fulfill based on their skills and availability to customers?

No.

What do you want to communicate with your channel?

I want to express that the entire organization services you and that we are available to help support you from the beginning to the end.

Describe how a network could apply to your idea.

This isn't applicable to me.

Is your core process standardizable or original work?

My core process is original work. This description is very helpful. I have spent a lot of time trying to force my process to be more like standardizable work. But, that is impossible, because we don't know what the solution looks like until we have it! This is a big load off my shoulders.

What methodology would help you improve quality?

We use all the latest methods in design and software development.

What metrics will you use to monitor performance?

The most important metrics for me are those that show how profitable each project is. Revenue growth is important but most important is the profit we generate on each contract. I have had some small contracts make more money than larger contracts because large contracts require a lot more time and resources, so if the terms were messed up in the beginning, then it only damages the company the more work we do under that contract.

What resources are critical for your plan?

Factor of Production	Description	Need
Capital	Tools and building	Low
Land	Natural resources	Low
Labor	Human efforts	High
Intellectual Property	Creations of the mind	Med
Time	Duration of the process	Med

Describe your output.

Technically I would say the output is the completion of projects.

Describe your fixed costs.

Not a lot of fixed costs. Corporate office, sales team, accounting, IT, and other necessary infrastructure.

Describe your variable costs.

Biggest variable cost is the employee's or contractor's time to complete the project.

Do you have an opportunity for economies of scale?

I don't have economies-of-scale business. Of course, the answer is sort of. If I call the brand a fixed cost that takes years to build, then maybe. The bigger we grow then the more money we make. But, I wouldn't say it is a high fixed costs business where the more you sell, the more you make per unit. You make a little more, but it is just a little bit more.

What is more important to you, rules or relationships?

Relationships are more important to me.

Do you prefer to work in a group or as an individual?

I prefer to work in a team. I do my best work on small iterations where we each work on something and then bring it back to the group. Most projects are built collaboratively with each person working on their piece, but it all has to fit together smoothly.

Do you display your emotions?

Yes, I show my emotions all the time. I am who I am, and my work is an expression of my personality and vision of what I contribute to the world. I need my emotions to be close so that I can create.

How separate do you keep your private and working life?

I like having a small circle of close friends. I like being close to the people I work with, but I don't usually have them come over to my house. I enjoy having a close culture, but I don't think they need to get involved in my personal life.

Do you have to prove yourself to receive status or is it given to you?

I think it is a combination of both. I like getting recognized for testing myself, but I also like the status for achieving certain things. I don't think I have to prove myself each time because my work requires inspiration and it doesn't always happen at the highest level each time.

Do you do things one at a time or several things at once?

I have to do several things at once. My projects have a lot of moving parts that I have to stay on top of all at once. Plus, when I am stuck on something creatively it helps me to work on something else and then come back to it. I can't force a good idea, but if I give it some time, then it will come on its own.

Do you control your environment or does your environment control you?

> *I think the setting controls me. I am just along for the ride and I try to do the best with whatever comes along.*

Who are the essentials you need in your hierarchy?

> *I need management to help me in the operations of the various pieces of the business. I want to grow a business based on the work that I do; I don't want to manage a growing business.*

How will you apply the rules of governance?

> *The clients we work with and the prices they are willing to pay dictate the level of talent in the market that we can hire to work with us. We can't hire the most talented people unless we are working with the clients with the largest budgets and who demand the highest quality. I will need to cultivate some essential clients so that I can manage the revenue in my organization to get the influentials I need.*

What is your vision for customer service?

> *I want to be a close partner with customers where we work on mission-critical projects.*

Review your analysis in the other types. Do you need to make any changes to your vision or your other types?

> *I need to improve our contract, on-boarding, and project-management process to better serve our clients.*

What combinations of types and grades of innovation would strengthen your idea?

> *I don't want to try complex coordination. All I need to do is create an industry standard business.*

Part 4: People

What expertise is required for your idea?

> *I need designers and software developers.*

Give one or more examples of extrinsic motivation for your idea.

> *Some people are driven to collect accolades and public recognition. Also, some people are always in search of the quick payday and the project that they can do quickly.*

Give one or more examples of intrinsic motivation for your idea.

> *For me, I like to create beautiful and useful things. For example, I paint during the weekends, and every few months I will have a show at an art gallery. I don't do it for the money or to become famous. I do it because I like to see my creations in the world and to see them appreciated by other people.*

What is the role for a creative in your idea?

> *Creatives are the most important piece of my idea. Essentially my idea is outsourced original work. Since this type of work is difficult for people to manage in their organizations, they turn to us to develop the solutions they need.*

What is the role for a systematic in your idea?

> *With so many creatives we need a systematic to help us manage the process, deliverables, communication with the customer, and billing and collections.*

What is the role for a bureaucrat in your idea?

> *I want to share assistants with the creative staff to make them more productive. There are a lot of tasks, such as time tracking, expense reports, travel, and status updates that I don't think creatives like doing or do well. We can have a systematic define the workflow and then we just need some bureaucrats to help us execute.*

Give me an example of a time you were in a mismatched role.

> *I worked for a year as an executive assistant for a family friend in his small business. I needed to find a job, and they needed help. I messed everything up.*

Do you have the right team for your idea?

> *I need a creative I trust to manage software development, and I need a systematic to help with sales and to create and document the standard operating procedures.*

Part 5: Organizational Structures

What structure is best for your idea?

> *Working inside a corporation could be possible, but I think all the creatives would eventually get bored working on the same types of projects. A startup company is perfect for my idea.*

Part 6: Diffusion Process

Who are your innovators?

> *Some clients want to push the boundaries of technology and explore what is possible. I have seen it with "big data" and now with "machine learning." Many people want to explore what is possible. These clients are a lot of fun to work with because their projects are more open and more undefined.*

Who are your early adopters?

> *Other clients need to use software to solve a business problem. These are the early adopters. But fortunately for business, in this industry, there are a lot of early majorities that see other companies developing software, and they all want to imitate them.*

Who are your industry non-adopters?

> *Some organizations are not incorporating custom software into their business and will never need us.*

Describe your target social system.

> *I just need to expand on my existing customer base. One social system of my current customer base is software development for construction companies. It is surprising that they do a lot of software development, but most of the software helps them operate and communicate internally, with other providers, and their clients. Software has a high value for them, they can price it into their contracts, and they can't manage any development internally.*

What are the social norms of your targeted social system?

> *All these guys know each other, and all compete for the same contracts, and employees move around from one company to*

another depending on who wins the big contract and needs the labor. So, they all compete, but they all respect each other. They care about the safety of their employees and their reputation.

How is the social system structured?

In my areas there is a top tier, middle tier, and lower tier.

How does the social system confer status?

Status is given to the bigger and more prestigious projects that they work on. Winning and building a museum with a famous architect confers more status than another apartment complex. But, a larger apartment complex confers more status than a smaller complex.

How does the social system gossip?

There are no secrets inside this group. Employees move around, and they all compete for the same projects, which can take a long time to negotiate and win and sometimes years to build. When we build software for one client, we can almost guarantee that next year we will develop similar software for another customer.

Sarah

Sarah walks in last. She smiles at me brightly, shakes my hand vigorously and says "Hi, David, great to finally meet you. Thanks for meeting with us today." I greet Sarah, and she sits in the middle chair, directly across from me. Sarah is dressed in a gray skirt, black flats, and a black long-sleeve shirt. Sarah has had a long career in technology, starting in 1996 with Netscape, after graduating from Wellesley College. She is currently data director of a startup helping news organizations generate sustainable membership-based revenue.

Part 1: Defining Innovation

Sarah, what is your favorite idea?

> *I want to create a unicorn. In my job I have interviewed, hired, and fired a lot of people. Due to all these interviews, I am better at interviewing than anyone I know. I believe that I have passed on good people who looked great on paper but did not interview well. I always used to think that they just didn't live up to their claimed experience and education. Before I was offered the management role with my current company, I went out to dinner with several other partners in the business. All of the partners are related, and I would be the first in senior management not a part of their family. At dinner, the partners asked me several questions about my children and my relationship with my husband. The questions they asked me were different than any others I have had before. I did fine answering these issues, but it got me thinking back to the people I have interviewed and the potentially good people whom I didn't hire. Were they qualified and would have made good employees but they were just not good at interviews? How many people have I passed over, just because they were not good at interviewing?*
>
> *So, I want to create an easy way for people to get the practice they desperately need. My idea is to have job seekers call in and*

interview with an experienced recruiter. The caller will receive a standard feedback form for each interview. As the job seeker calls in more, he gets more feedback and can track the progress. The caller pays a per-minute fee, and I add the charge to their phone bill.

I look at startups like Monster.com, Indeed.com, and LinkedIn. These companies built their businesses around job hunters, and I think it is a huge market with potential.

How has reasoning by analogy guided your idea?

Well, if I understand it correctly, I would say that the part about how I plan to charge. If I need to make someone sign up on the website and enter their credit card all before they call, then my conversion rates will be very low. So, I remembered the old 1-900 numbers that used to be used for phone sex. People would call the numbers and talk to a woman on the phone. The caller would pay a charge on their phone bill. So, I figured if people could just call my recruiters and we charge through their phone bill, then I get to avoid the entire sign-up and credit card process.

How have you used reasoning by first principles on your idea?

I have never heard of this before. I didn't use first principles. Well, maybe I didn't do it consciously, but perhaps I used the process without knowing it at the time. Can practice be reasoning by first principles? To improve anything people need to practice. I want to help people enhance their interviewing skills. So, this means that they need practice. My idea is just providing an easy way to for them to practice.

What problem do you want to solve?

I want to improve interviewees' interview skills.

What constraints have prevented solving the problem?

Job seeking is an occasional activity for interviewees, so the interview skills are under-developed. Companies have no incentive to provide training to a broad employee base.

Recruiters usually work finding people for open positions, except for high-level positions.

What is your industry?

Job searching and recruiting.

What is your "valuable order"?

Allow job searchers to quickly and inexpensively receive consistent interview feedback.

What do you expect is the most difficult "internal disorder" problem you need to solve?

Sourcing skilled interviewers.

What do you expect is the most difficult "external disorder" problem you need to solve?

Reaching job searchers at the right time.

Part 2: Innovation Grades

Define AAA grade for your industry.

Trailing industry standards is self-study on how to find a job and improve interviewing skills. Many job seekers read articles online or buy a book.

Is now the right time?

Job search industry mirrors the general economy. When the economy is strong, people feel more confident and are more likely to change jobs. When the economy is weak, people are more scared and usually stay with a job they have. I think things are stable now.

Define AA grade for your industry.

Recruiters are the industry standard. The hiring company announces or contracts with a recruiter who then finds candidates and prescreens them. Recruiters select the candidates they would like to present and prepare the candidates for the interviews with additional information regarding the client and the position.

Do you have a way not just to create but deliver your product?

> I can deliver the services through the phones, which is a big part of the service. I would look to how companies attract new hires and advertise through the same channels, the Internet, recruiters, job fairs, and recruiters.

Define A grade for your industry.

> I think this grade is the personal consultants helping provide customized advice and support to job seekers. These can be very expensive and are usually only for executives. There are not very many open positions, relatively, so competition for those jobs is intense, and the margins for the consultants can be very high because they are like professional sports agents.

Will your market position be defensible 10 and 20 years into the future?

> It might not be. This question highlights that my idea is a feature and a foundation of a business, but it is incomplete to sustain. If the idea is successful, it would likely mean that we will have to diversify and become involved in industry standard services, such as job placements or temporary staffing.

Define B grade for your industry.

> I think our industry could learn from online schools that allow remote access and instruction. There are important skill sets to communicating with resumes and interviewing, but there isn't an industry-leading way that teaches people how and what they should be doing. I could envision an online "school" that offers courses in resume building, networking, interviewing, and other valuable job searching skills.

Do you have the right team?

> I don't have the right team to build a curriculum on job searching. I am missing someone who could help bridge the gap in creating courses that would instruct and assess progress. I would need someone from a school district or a university.
>
> I do have the right team to build the service I envision. I think if we expand to standard recruiting and placement services then I would need an industry insider to bring on as a partner.

Is there a group that has historically been underfunded, understaffed, and as a result has gone without? Is this group likely to appreciate lower cost "good enough" solutions?

> *People entering the job market, such as the young and immigrants, are underserved. They have low resources and little experience. Recruiters can't do anything with them usually. High-end recruiters definitely can't do anything with them. So, they are left on their own not receiving any help.*

Is it possible to be profitable while providing the solution?

> *Maybe. If this is my strategy, to target the underserved, I would have to figure out if I can contract with professional interviewers while keeping my fees low enough. But, the most difficult challenge may be how to reach the customers. How I advertise and inform those underserved may be very expensive.*

Have you identified an opportunity others don't see?

> *I see a problem and an opportunity. What I don't know is if this underserved group sees value in the service.*

Can you create a 10x improvement with no close substitute?

> *No, I don't see what a 10x solution would look like in this market. I don't think my idea is 10x better.*

Could your idea create or face any new regulations?

> *No.*

Part 3: Innovation Types

Describe buyer motivations for your product and the five product characteristics.

Consumption:

> *I think this is the weakest motivation. My prospects could use the service to improve their interview and communication skills because they see this area as a source of deficiency.*

Investment:

> *The strongest motivation for my service is an investment. Prospects will want to spend money on improving their*

interview skills when they are ready to start looking for a job so that they can get better job offers.

Saving:

Prospects can be motivated to save time in their job search. The better they perform on their interviews, the quicker they can get an offer. These candidates are not worried about getting an offer; they are concerned about getting an offer as quickly as possible.

Insurance:

Some potential prospects will see improving their interview skills as a way to ensure that they have all their bases covered. They might not think that it will help, but they will do it, just in case it might assist them to get an offer.

Negative Value:

A prospect can be afraid that he pays and then doesn't get anything out of it. Or, maybe they pick up some interview habit that makes them worse at interviewing.

Describe how you can improve your product based on the five product characteristics:

Relative Advantage:

Practicing interviewing is currently difficult. Finding someone you trust, coordinating a time and location, and then the feedback is inconsistent, and you only have one person's perspective. Picking up the phone and calling, doing an interview, getting the emailed report and paying through phone bill is a vast improvement.

Compatibility:

I think the key here is to be compatible with the existing job-hunting process. Needs to feel a natural part of the job boards and recruiters. Recruiters should be recommending everyone use this service to prepare for job interviews.

Complexity:

I think complexity for me means the ease to sign up for the service. I can get it close to Amazon's One-Click Checkout.

> Prospects just call our 1-900 number, and we charge the phone bill. The interviewer asks for the email address during the interview to send the report. I will need to make sure the report is also straightforward and easy to understand.

Trialability:
> I think this means that it is better to have a free trial? I can easily provide the first interview for free. I will have to plan those acquisitions costs into my financial model. I will have to provide a 1-800 number and then cover the expenses of the person conducting the interview.

Observability:
> This one I don't think that I can do very well. I guess the best I can do here is to have testimonials of job hunters and how the service helped them.

Describe how you could use each of the four funding sources.

Equity:
> I will use equity with cofounders, and a little for some early employees. We will likely have to raise money from investors.

Revenue:
> The value is given to the interviewee, so they should pay for the service.

Government:
> Maybe there are some government grants to help pay for job preparation training, such as for military veterans or former prison inmates.

Donations:
> If there isn't government funding, perhaps I could pursue cash donations to help pay for the veterans. Also, I think maybe there is an opportunity for the interviewers to donate their time for several of the Wikipedia reasons. So, perhaps I could reduce my interview costs.

Which funding source will you focus on?

> *I had not considered donations as an important piece of my plans, but I think there is something to having interviewers be from existing companies. For example, a large tech company such as Google might provide some HR personnel time to interview specific prospects. Worst case scenario, the interviewer provides useful feedback and best case scenario, the interviewer has identified a potential candidate to bring back in for another interview with the company. This could change my model a little bit, in that I won't have to pay recruiters or other HR professionals to conduct the interview. Something I need to think about too is maybe I could charge Google to allow their staff to do the interviews. If I am using their employees, all of a sudden, I am creating value to both sides of the interview. But my main funding source will be revenue for the interview services and equity to help fund the growth.*

Describe how you could use information dissemination and information accumulation with your product.

> *This has made me think that perhaps there is an additional business line in the future. If we can accumulate a lot of information about a candidate's background, ability to improve in a job interview, but also include our technical assessment of their skills, such as a software coding assessment, we could begin to advise medium-sized companies on their hiring practices.*
>
> *For example, a medium-sized company might know what they want in a candidate, but they might not be as good at assessing and selecting candidates. Their selection process might be flawed, due to their internal interview process and how they rank candidates due to the results of their interview process. We could use our information to help them identify the ideal candidate.*
>
> *The information we can capture and integrate could also be made free to our customers. They will want to know how they compare to other similar interviewees and how they progress about their peers. We can share all this information with them.*

What impression do you want to convey with your brand?

The impression I want people to have with my brand is that they have a partner in the job search. I want my customers to feel like this isn't just a transaction, but that we care about them and like we are part of their team while they are searching. I want them not to feel alone.

Describe how customers in your industry want your brand to make others perceive them.

People want to appear prepared and professional. I want people to be proud that people know they use my service and not embarrassed. If my customers don't want people to know that they used us, then that is not good for us.

Describe what your brand makes customers feel about themselves.

People want to confirm to themselves that they have personal value during this process.

Highlight your brand personalities.

Personality	High	Low
Conscientiousness	**Efficient, Hard-working, Well-organized**	Easy-Going, Negligent, Lazy, Disorganized
Agreeableness	**Friendly, Trusting, Lenient**	Analytical, Ruthless, Critical
Neuroticism	Nervous, Emotional, Worried	**Confident, Unemotional, Calm**
Openness	Curious, Creative, Imaginative	**Cautious, Conventional, Down-to-earth**
Extraversion	**Outgoing, Talkative, Active**	Reserved, Loner, Quiet

What are your industry's standard direct and indirect channels?

I think to look at it this way, recruiters are the indirect channels, and the direct channels are individuals working their personal network to get introductions to job opportunities.

What is your direct channel approach?

> *Our direct approach will be through the advertising on the web for prospects to call us and try out the service. Eventually, if we expand to offer recruiting services, we will compete with indirect channels.*

Is the sales process documented and can it easily be communicated to sales people?

> *Yes, I can do this easily. I know how to create a sales system.*

Is there an existing demand that partners can fulfill based on their skills and availability to customers?

> *I have a lot of sales experience, and recruiters get paid on commissions. They want a product that is ready. If they send a candidate that isn't ready, not only do they miss out on commission but they also risk damaging their reputation with their client.*

Describe potential indirect channel, alliance, and influencer relationships.

> *I want recruiters to see us as a free service (to them) to help their candidates be better prepared. From a recruiter standpoint, they get a better-prepared candidate, which means higher close rates and faster commissions.*

What do you want to communicate with your channel?

> *I want to communicate that people who are serious about their job search use the interview preparation to get ready.*

Describe how a network could apply to your idea.

> *I don't think that I have a network opportunity. There are some aspects of a network, but I don't think the value to any user of my customers improves with more users. Maybe if I changed my idea, but I want to help the job-seekers, not recruiters or companies directly.*

Is your core process standardizable or original work?

> *My process is 100 percent standardizable. It is standardized assessment, which is valuable and comparable from one interview to the next.*

What methodology would help you improve quality?

> *The lean ideas will assist in making and developing our assessment on an ongoing basis.*

What metrics will you use to monitor performance?

> *My focus will be on various revenue metrics. This is my bread and butter. It is all about the good leads and how we convert those leads into customers.*

What resources are critical for your plan?

Factor of Production	Description	Need
Capital	Tools and building	Low
Land	Natural resources	Low
Labor	Human efforts	High
Intellectual Property	Creations of the mind	Medium
Time	Duration of the process	Medium

Describe your output.

> *My output is the interview assessment reports.*

Describe your fixed costs.

> *I don't have a lot of fixed costs. They are primarily the enabling process, all the corporate structure and the original systems to receive calls, route them, and the original interview assessment.*

Describe your variable costs.

> *I get to match revenue to most expenses. My variable costs are customer acquisition costs and interview costs.*

Do you have an opportunity for economies of scale?

> *No, I don't think so.*

What is more important to you, rules or relationships?

> *Relationships. I love top performers, and I treat people I work with like family.*

Do you prefer to work in a group or as an individual?

I prefer to work as an individual. I like when I work with people that are good at what they do and can specialize in their domain.

Do you display your emotions?

I am not emotional, except when I am pissed off or excited and happy.

How separate do you keep your private and working life?

I completely mix the two. My best friends are my coworkers, and I like to recruit my friends to come and work with me.

Do you have to prove yourself to receive status or is it given to you?

I want to prove myself every day. I want those I work with to show themselves. I have had to fire some people with fantastic experience, but if they don't perform, there is no room for them.

Do you do things one at a time or several things at once?

I do one thing at a time. I prefer to be laser focused on something and to do well on that thing and then to move on to the next.

Do you control your environment or does your environment control you?

I think you control your environment—but you need to pick the situation you know you can control.

Who are the essentials you need in your hierarchy?

I know that I will need to raise some money so those are the essentials. I will give some equity to other team members, but I want to be in charge in the company. I am good at managing people, and I add the most value in the company because I can sell, and at the end of the day, these are the two most important qualities in the hierarchy. I can govern from the top and make sure that the organization is well run and people are getting their work done. So everyone else I see as influentials, not as essentials.

How will you apply the rules of governance?

> *I see the largest risk of not being able to control my own destiny in the revenue. I think there is a risk of gaining one essential customer early in the process. While that is great for revenue we would customize the experience to that customer, because their revenue is so important. That influence on our product will put the entire organization at risk if we lose that customer. I will need to make sure that I add smaller interchangeable customers.*

What is your vision for customer service?

> *I think the key is what I want the brand impression to be. The impression I want people to have with my brand is that they have a partner in the job search. I want my customers to feel like this isn't just a transaction, but that we care about them and like we are part of their team while they are searching. I want them not to feel alone.*

Review your analysis in the other types. Do you need to make any changes to your vision or your other types?

> *No, I don't think so.*

What combinations of types and grades of innovation would strengthen your idea?

> *I don't think that any complex coordination is possible with my idea and the way that I work.*

Part 4: People

What expertise is required for your idea?

> *My idea depends on being able to generate the sales channels and sell the product, it requires expertise in creating the interview assessments, the technical skills to manage the phone calls and the back-end system for those conducting the interviews to record their notes to send to the client.*

Give one or more examples of extrinsic motivation for your idea.

> *Making money motivates me. I like to earn money, and this idea can be huge, measured by revenue and in valuation. This is a startup idea that is scalable and can be sustained by revenue. It is a real business.*

Give one or more examples of intrinsic motivation for your idea.

I want to help job-seekers improve their interview skills to express clearly who they are. It sincerely bothers me when candidates and companies use a misleading interview to assess a good match.

What is the role for a creative in your idea?

I need creatives for crafting the technical solutions and the interview assessments. Those things right now are "original work" that we need to solve. I don't need creatives once we are up and running.

What is the role for a systematic in your idea?

I need systematics to create the internal processes to manage.

What is the role for a bureaucrat in your idea?

Most of the work once I have a working solution will be done by "bureaucrats," such as sales, the interviewers, and maintaining all the internal processes.

Give me an example of a time you were in a mismatched role.

I am a systematic. I like creating order and systems and improving critical processes. When I first started my career in the family company, I started in sales, where I didn't have any power to change or improve anything. I had to work for a manager who was good at doing what he was told but didn't have a vision or ambition to improve things. There was a lot I had to learn about the products we sold and sales techniques, but it was torture working a sales process that I knew I could improve.

Do you have the right team for your idea?

I am not sure that I have the right creative team. They are profoundly influential in the beginning, but I don't want to give them tons of equity to help launch something when I don't need them on an ongoing basis. Also, I will need to recruit someone to make our interview assessments.

Part 5: Organizational Structures

What structure is best for your idea?

I think a startup is the best place for the idea. It could be a feature for a recruiting company, but it wouldn't have the legs to be able to grow to job-seekers working with other recruiters.

Part 6: Diffusion Process

Who are your innovators?

I am not sure. I am not doing anything particularly difficult technically.

Who are your early adopters?

Those that need to improve their interview skills the most are those that are professionals, but where there is still significant competition and where their professional networks and track records are not entirely developed. For example, college graduates with less than five years work experience need to be able to take advantage any time they can secure an interview. I think it would be best for me to focus on the major metropolitan areas, where there are a lot of candidates and always a lot of open positions.

Who are your industry non-adopters?

I think blue-collar or minimum wage workers are my industry non-adopters.

Describe your target social system.

My target system is what I see as early adopters. Young professionals with less than five years professional experience in major metro areas.

What are the social norms of your targeted social system?

The young professionals are at a stage where they are building a network, need to change companies to advance their careers, they value collaboration, taking risks, and growing their expertise.

How is the social system structured?

> *The social systems are organized by technical expertise. Accountants, lawyers, computer hardware, computer software, and salespeople. They are also structured inside the companies and departments.*
>
> *This point makes me realize that I should focus on a niche domain and geographic area in the beginning. Such as accounting in New York and software developers in San Francisco.*

How does the social system confer status?

> *Young professionals confer status to those that can develop strong technical abilities in their domain and can take advantage of opportunities with projects or positions.*

How does the social system gossip?

> *There is a lot of gossip inside companies about the performance of co-workers. The social groups also communicate through friends, alumni associations, professional groups, and other networking events.*

Joko

Joko is an Indonesian immigrant and a Stanford graduate with a dual degree in computer science and linguistics. He makes brief eye contact, smiles and sits down immediately in the chair on my right. As I get to know Joko better I realize that he is one the most intelligent people I have ever met. He is wearing a pair of light blue denim pants, a white long-sleeve button-up dress shirt, and a pair of black Nike running shoes. Joko works for a fast-growing company that recently held its initial public offering. It provides software to Fortune 500 companies.

Part 1: Defining Innovation

Joko, what is your favorite idea?

I have learned that the sound of a person's voice will tell me if he is saying something important — at least to him. For the past few years, I have been tinkering with some software that I started writing in college to help me study for my classes. I recorded the professors' lectures and combined them with the textbooks and the exam questions and the correct and incorrect answers. Over time my software has learned to suggest a study guide based on the materials the professors would talk about in their lectures, including the inflections in their voices, compared to the exam question and answers. The software suggests the most relevant sections from the textbooks and other reading materials. I have improved the algorithms over time, and several people started using the software to study and get better grades. The software was helpful in school, and I think it must have a commercial application, even though I am not sure exactly what that use might be. For sure, it helps students in higher education. With the right tweaks, it could help the NSA filter through the data it collects to prevent the next terrorist attack. Maybe investors could use it to prevent the next Enron fraud by comparing the calls with management to all the financial disclosures. I am sure there are some other uses. Maybe my software could interpret verbal cues for a larger artificial intelligence system. Honestly, I am not sure what the best or future use will be.

Can you explain how reasoning by analogy has shaped your idea?

There are many contributing factors, but one thing that helped inspire me was playing around with Apple's Siri. I liked that Siri could listen to a voice and appear to make sense of the question. Sometimes when Siri doesn't have an answer, it just does an Internet search. So, the first few versions of my software were able to capture what a professor said and query the readings and exams to match the text. Those first versions took me far, even though the secret sauce would come later when I started weighting based on the verbal emphasis.

How do you incorporate first principles in your planning?

For me first principles are part of the algorithms I wrote to analyze the sound of a person's voice to tell me if he is saying something important. I broke down the voice by hertz and the pace of the speech compared to other examples of speech from that person. Only by using the basic principles of speech could I break it down to reveal the secrets of what the person who was speaking considers most important.

What problem do you want to solve?

Being able to analyze human conversations to provide actionable insights hidden from human ears and recollection.

What constraints have prevented solving the problem?

The processing power and the connecting nuances in the voice to the meaning and relevant data.

What is your industry?

Artificial intelligence.

What is your "valuable order"?

Intelligent speech recognition and query of content related to the conversation.

What do you expect is the most difficult "internal disorder" problem you need to solve?

> *How the software scales will be the most difficult problem. It will be hard to use the software to analyze increasingly complex conversations and increasingly less related content.*

What do you expect is the most difficult "external disorder" problem you need to solve?

> *I think the biggest problem will be the network we connect to, meaning what we connect to other data, other systems, or with other artificial intelligence providers.*

Part 2: Innovation Grades

Define AAA grade for your industry.

> *For my idea, Grade AAA standards are basic transcription services or software. Radiology uses transcription to convert the physicians' verbal diagnosis from MRIs and x-rays to text that ends up in a patient record. This technology just changes the audio to text. Several companies provide transcription software. For the past few years radiology reimbursements have been getting cut, so I know that declining revenue has put stress on software providers in that sector.*

Is now the right time?

> *It is. We are at a time when we have enough processing power and Internet bandwidth to begin, and we can expect capacity to improve to meet our needs in the future.*

Define AA grade for your industry.

> *Grade AA now is software designed to take basic human interactions and respond with preprogrammed answers. I think of it like calling into a phone system for a credit card company. Software routes your call through the limited voice prompted options, such as "make a payment" or "customer service."*

Do you have a way not just to create but deliver your product?

> *The distribution process for Grade AA kind of business to business software is expensive and time-consuming. I think there*

is a way to evolve by focusing on some consumer services that employees bring into the enterprise. Some startups like Box and Dropbox that have figured out how to make that transition.

Define A grade for your industry.

The difference between Grade AA and Grade A is pretty big. Grade A is Apple's Siri, Amazon's Echo, and Google's Home. This software is the current leading industry standard for voice recognition. The competition here is very intense. Apple, Amazon, and Google are all competing. Each of these three companies is growing quickly, has existing distribution channels, and can practically dedicate whatever resources they require to develop the technology.

Will your market position be defensible 10 and 20 years into the future?

If my technology remains static then it won't be sustainable because others will be able to replicate the functionality. The market position could be defensible if my technology continues to improve and we can dominate a niche before others can catch up.

Define B grade for your industry.

What artificial intelligence is trying to do is imitate nature. We are seeking to understand the neural networks and how they work so that we can recreate them with computers. There is a quote I like: "Any sufficiently advanced technology is indistinguishable from magic." Right now there is some "magic" that happens inside the brain. Eventually, we will understand how the technology works or replicate our design.

Do you have the right team?

There is a high team risk in artificial intelligence. I think that an engineering team is handicapped when approaching AI because they see learning as a design problem, primarily a mathematical equation. Some teams are involving neurologists now because they can provide some context to the way the brain develops. The way a child learns is understood by neuroscience, but it

> isn't the best way to teach a child. Have you ever met a neurologist? Would you want them to be a preschool teacher? Do you expect them to create a curriculum for a four-year-old? I have never met a neurologist that I would want to be a preschool teacher. Ask a preschool teacher how a child learns, and their perspective will be very different than a neurologist's perspective. So, when we are teaching computers how to learn perhaps the teams need to involve input from a variety of perspectives. Can a preschool teacher help an AI team create a curriculum for a computer based on their understanding of how a four-year-old child learns?

Is there a group that has historically been underfunded, understaffed, and as a result has gone without? Is this group likely to appreciate lower cost "good enough" solutions?

> Yes, the industry is still young, but students are usually underserved and do not have the resources for analytics, artificial intelligence, or speech analysis to help them study.

Is it possible to be profitable while providing the solution?

> I think so. The software is scalable and improves with more data. The distribution should be relatively inexpensive since we could target individual schools at a time and students live close to each other.

Have you identified an opportunity others don't see?

> Well, no one else is pursuing the idea in this manner. Who wants to sell to students when this could be refined and sold to banks, Wall Street firms, hedge funds, and governments? But, I could start with students and then as the software improves I can move up market to the more lucrative opportunities.

Can you create a 10x improvement with no close substitute?

> Maybe. I think what I have built has no close substitute. It has a lot of potential, but there is a lot of work to do. Artificial Intelligence would certainly be a Decade innovation. It is not impossible and eventually someone will discover it. It is already not popular and some people want to prevent it and certainly

> there is already a fear of AI. But, AI will be the most valuable invention the world has seen. If it is created by a private individual, the invention will make them the richest person in the world—if they can avoid the regulation. I don't want to claim that I am creating AI, but layering what I have created can help the AI understand humans better.

Could your idea create or face any new regulations?

> Yes. I don't know what the regulations should be, but AI will definitely face regulations.

Part 3: Innovation Types

Describe buyer motivations for your product and the five product characteristics.

Consumption:

> I will focus on the student market, because I know the most about it. Students can use the software to study and improve their grades and understanding of the material.

Investment:

> Students will see the software as an investment because they are spending a lot of money in college and spending a little extra on this software returns much better grades.

Saving:

> Students I let use the software saw that it saved them a lot of time by focusing on the most important course material.

Insurance:

> There was one friend who used the software just to make sure that she wasn't missing something from the lectures or the readings.

Negative Value:

> An early software version miscalculated the emphasis from a British professor and so I studied the wrong chapters and flunked an important exam.

Describe how you can improve your product based on the five product characteristics:

Relative Advantage:
> *There is no close substitute. What I have created is the best study guide ever invented.*

Compatibility:
> *The software is compatible with current technology.*

Complexity:
> *The software is very easy to use and takes a few minutes to learn.*

Trialability:
> *I can easily let students try the software. In school, anyone who tried it was almost immediately addicted.*

Observability:
> *It isn't the most observable software, but in a classroom during a semester every other student learned about what I was doing.*

Describe how you could use each of the four funding sources.

Equity:
> *My idea will definitely require significant investment and the regular stock options.*

Revenue:
> *The product works well and people will be willing to pay for it. Even poor students are willing to pay for it.*

Government:
> *I am sure the government would be interested in the technology and would contract with us, once we can demonstrate that it would work for them. Or, maybe if we could get the right contacts, they might be willing to help us develop government capabilities.*

Donations:
> *Maybe I could "crowd-source" some recorded audio to improve my dataset.*

Which funding source will you focus on?
> *Most likely equity and revenue will be important in the beginning and government might become more important as the*

software gets more sophisticated. I am conflicted about using government money because it can keep people safe but it can also be used to spy on an innocent population.

Describe how you could use information dissemination and information accumulation with your product.

My algorithm is powerful, and I process a lot of data. I think we are accumulating the information because it is very valuable to our insights. As time goes on, the algorithm improves as there are more ways an individual can verbally communicate what they think about what they are saying. Additionally, the more accents and languages we include then the better the results will be over time.

I don't think we could disseminate our information, but we could disseminate the analysis of the data. For example, we can take public data, such as everything a politician says publicly, analyze it and then share the results with the world. I am not sure that we will ever be able to say if a politician is lying, but we could provide other context like whether what they are saying is important to them or not. If a politician says that he really wants a healthcare bill to be voted on and passed by Congress, we could tell you whether he felt confident about that or not.

What impression do you want to convey with your brand?

I want people to be in awe of technology. I know that feeling will change over time as it becomes more commonplace, but I want people to embrace advanced technology and not be afraid. I want them to feel like it is magical.

Describe how customers in your industry want your brand to make others perceive them.

Students want to be perceived as smart and hard-working and they want the software to reinforce the perception.

Describe what your brand makes customers feel about themselves.

Students want to feel prepared.

Highlight your brand personalities.

Personality	High	Low
Conscientiousness	**Efficient, Hard-working, Well-organized**	Easy-Going, Negligent, Lazy, Disorganized
Agreeableness	Friendly, Trusting, Lenient	**Analytical, Ruthless, Critical**
Neuroticism	Nervous, Emotional, Worried	**Confident, Unemotional, Calm**
Openness	**Curious, Creative, Imaginative**	Cautious, Conventional, Down-to-earth
Extraversion	Outgoing, Talkative, Active	**Reserved, Loner, Quiet**

What are your industry's standard direct and indirect channels?

There are software companies that can benefit from indirect channels, especially those companies that sell to other businesses. But I think all of my distribution will come through a website and most marketing will be by word of mouth and the media talking about the technology.

Is the sales process documented and can it easily be communicated to sales people?

No.

Is there an existing demand that partners can fulfill based on their skills and availability to customers?

No.

What do you want to communicate with your channel?

I want to communicate that the technology is so good that users will come to us.

Describe a closed standard/compatible network for your idea.

I think this type of network is what I had envisioned. I want to control the technology but make it available and compatible with current hardware and software.

Describe a closed standard/compatible network for your idea.

I think this type of network is what I had envisioned. I want to control the technology but make it available and compatible with current hardware and software.

Describe a closed standard/incompatible network for your idea.

If I were to make it incompatible with existing networks I think it would mean that I would develop my own hardware. The downside of this is students would have to buy new hardware and I would have to design and manufacture the hardware. I had to think for a long time about the benefits of building incompatibility. When we talked about the product one of the weaknesses was that the solution was not really observable. But, if students had to come to class and put a device on their desk to record the lecture, it would make it much more visible. I don't know if the trade-off is worth it because of all the problems we might have getting into hardware. Maybe it would make the software look cooler if it needed its own hardware, but if anyone opened up the box they would see a fairly basic recording device.

Describe an open standard/compatible network for your idea.

Making the software open could be interesting. Perhaps I could open up the algorithm as a platform for other developers to incorporate. I don't want to do this because it means I could lose control over the technology.

Describe an open standard/incompatible network for your idea.

This type of network doesn't really make sense for my idea. I would make it open and incompatible with existing technology? Seems that would make it much more difficult to adopt. I am not iterating on an existing capability.

Is your core process standardizable or original work?

My core process is original work. I don't even know what I can build on top of the algorithms or how users will use it.

What methodology would help you improve quality?

I think in the future all of the methodologies you described will be helpful. But, for now all I need to do is work on improving the technology. I only need a small team right now because I don't want to spend any time trying to coordinate, I just want us to focus on building and improving the capabilities.

What metrics will you use to monitor performance?

The most important metrics for me are about how many users are using the software and the amount of data we are able to process. Active users will drive valuation. The data we have will help improve the technology.

What resources are critical for your plan?

Factor of Production	Description	Need
Capital	Tools and building	Low
Land	Natural resources	Low
Labor	Human efforts	High
Intellectual Property	Creations of the mind	High
Time	Duration of the process	High

Describe your output.

The output is insight to spoken language and connection to other data. My software has learned to suggest a study guide based on the materials the professors would talk about in their lectures, including the inflections in their voices, compared to the exam questions and answers. The software suggests the most important sections from the textbooks and other reading materials. I have improved the algorithms over time and several people started using the software to study and get better grades.

Describe your fixed costs.

> *Software development is a huge fixed cost, especially to improve the software and take it to the highest output possible in other contexts.*

Describe your variable costs.

> *Variable costs are just computing costs and they are very small compared to the fixed costs.*

Do you have an opportunity for economies of scale?

> *Definitely I have an opportunity for economies of scale.*

What is more important to you, rules or relationships?

> *Rules are more important to me. I want to find truth and how things are designed to operate and then follow those guidelines to achieve the desired result.*

Do you prefer to work in a group or as individual?

> *It depends on the type of work. Usually I prefer to work alone because I can produce the best code when I am at home alone. But, I know that I have to work with other people to get other things done.*

Do you display your emotions?

> *Not really. I prefer to keep these things to myself.*

How separate do you keep your private and working life?

> *I usually keep things separate. I like to have different aspects of my life.*

Do you have to prove yourself to receive status or is it given to you?

> *I think you have to prove yourself. Technology changes quickly, so you have to keep up or be left behind.*

Do you do things one at a time or several things at once?

> *I do best when I can focus in on one thing for days or weeks at a time.*

Do you control your environment or does your environment control you?

> *I think we are all just going with the flow of whatever life brings us. I think we can choose how we react, but even our reactions, choices, and preferences were all dictated by an environment*

that we can't control. I am just the result of an environment I didn't choose.

Who are the essentials you need in your hierarchy?

I need someone to help guide me in navigating the commercialization of the software. I know it works for students, but I don't know what other applications it will have or how to sell it.

How will you apply the rules of governance?

I don't think I need to be concerned too much in the beginning because the most important thing is the technology. However, I am afraid that over time the highest bidder will decide how it is applied. For example, I don't want the technology to be used for spying on political opponents, even though that might be very lucrative. We also will need to be careful about our partners because if we incorporate other technology it might limit what customers we can serve or it might make us lazy in developing our own technology.

What is your vision for customer service?

I don't want any interaction with customers. I want the technology to just work for them so they have no reason to contact me.

Review your analysis in the other types. Do you need to make any changes to your vision or to your other types?

No, I don't need to make any changes.

What combinations of types and grades of innovation would strengthen your idea?

This is an interesting concept. I have just thought that the product would be all that I need to worry about. But I think the most important types are the product, information, brand, and hierarchy. I will need to carefully manage these other aspects with the product.

Part 4: People

What expertise is required for your idea?

> *Overall for my entire vision, you need expertise in natural language processing, machine learning, linear algebra, calculus, probability and statistics, and neurology, neuroplasticity, and the human brain.*

Give one or more examples of extrinsic motivation for your idea.

> *Some people are driven by money or fame. I am afraid some people are motivated by infamy.*

Give one or more examples of intrinsic motivation for your idea.

> *I know this is an over-used motivation, but I want technology to improve the world. Most people in the world just want to live a happy life and technology is the key to improving the living conditions and the lives of millions of people around the world.*

What is the role for a creative in your idea?

> *We are working to solve something that has never been done before, so all the work is original and we need a lot of creatives. I have seen some people with the required expertise, but they are actually just bureaucrats, people who can only do what they are told.*

What is the role for a systematic in your idea?

> *I think a systematic is helpful to make things more useful for an end-user. Usually, I am so focused on solving a technical problem that it is hard for me to empathize with an end-user.*

What is the role for a bureaucrat in your idea?

> *I don't know if there is a role for a bureaucrat for some time. I don't like to work with people who can only do what they have been told. It is frustrating.*

Give me an example of a time you were in a mismatched role.

> *In my first job out of college I was working through updating and maintaining legacy code and 90 percent of my time was spent fixing bugs and not developing new features. This also*

meant a lot of time on documentation. I hated it, and I learned nothing new. Eventually, I was moved to work on other projects. If I had stayed on those first projects for much longer, I would have quit.

Do you have the right team for your idea?

I thought that I just needed a designer to make things look good and a sales guy to go out and sell. But, to focus on the technology, I need to raise some money and hire creatives with the expertise to take the software to the next level.

Part 5: Organizational Structures

What structure is best for your idea?

I think in a startup we would have the flexibility to go wherever the technology takes us. But, in a larger company we would have more resources and could focus on the technology and not some of the business aspects, such as running the company and raising money. I think a startup is the best place, but if Google or Apple wanted to support us and give us autonomy, I would say yes.

Part 6: Diffusion Process

Who are your innovators?

Our innovators are those that like the technology and find what we are working on is really cool. I have a lot of friends that love to play around with the algorithm and see what they can do with it. One friend recorded the presidential debate between Trump and Clinton. I thought the results were interesting.

Who are your early adopters?

The software solves a problem for students and it does better than anything else that I am aware of. Students love it and need it.

Who are your industry non-adopters?

Who would never adopt the technology? I think we are close to an inflection point where AI and neural lace will redefine what it means to be human and many people will begin to reject technology to live a more traditional human life. In other words, I think humans will integrate computers and computers will become more humanlike and the line will become blurry where one starts and another end. I can see a lot of people just wanting to live a traditional human life.

Describe your target social system.

I want to start with university students because I understand them and I know the software works. I can continue to improve the software for them and for other commercial uses.

What are the social norms of your targeted social system?

University students are optimistic about the future, they value progress and knowledge. They are digital natives and are comfortable using new technology in any aspect of their life. Students also have a strange combination of collaboration and competition.

How is the social system structured?

There are a couple of different structures in student life based on how students interact with each other. There are systems based on academic departments, sororities and fraternities, individual classes, housing, and of course other living arrangements, either in the dorms or off campus.

How does the social system confer status?

Student social systems confer status a little different depending on how or why it is structured. I think primarily those students who are naturally smarter and work hard are respected. I also think students that work on something outside of their coursework have higher status.

How does the social system gossip?

Students gossip all the time on social media, in study groups, and in their extracurricular activities. Student life is fairly well connected, so when something happens it can spread quickly.

Questionnaire

Part 1: Defining Innovation

What is your favorite idea?

How reasoning by analogy has shaped your idea?

Can you incorporate first principles in your planning?

What problem do you want to solve?

What constraints have prevented solving the problem?

What is your industry?

What is your "valuable order"?

What do you expect is the most difficult "internal disorder" problem you need to solve?

What do you expect is the most difficult "external disorder" problem you need to solve?

Part 2: Innovation Grades

Define AAA grade, trailing industry standards, for your industry.

Is now the right time?

Define AA grade, industry standard, for your industry.

Do you have a way not just to create but deliver your product?

Define A grade, leading industry standards, for your industry.

Will your market position be defensible 10 and 20 years into the future?

Define B grade, Mimetic, for your industry.

Do you have the right team?

Explore C grade, the Wave, for your industry. Is there a group that has historically been underfunded, understaffed, and as a result has gone without? Is this group likely to appreciate lower cost "good enough" solutions?

Is it possible to be profitable while providing the solution?

Have you identified an opportunity others don't see?

Explore D grade, Decade, for your industry. Can you create a 10x improvement with no close substitute?

Part 3: Innovation Types

Describe buyer motivations for your product and the five product characteristics.
- Consumption:
- Investment:
- Saving:
- Insurance:
- Negative Value:

Describe how you can improve your product based on the five product characteristics:
- Relative Advantage:
- Compatibility:

- Complexity:
- Trialability:
- Observability:

Describe how you could use each of the four funding sources.
- Equity:
- Revenue:
- Government:
- Donations:
- Which funding source will you focus on?

Describe how you could use information dissemination and information accumulation with your product.

What impression do you want to convey with your brand?

Describe how customers in your industry want your brand to make others perceive them.

Describe what your brand makes customers feel about themselves.

Highlight your brand personalities.

Personality	High	Low
Conscientiousness	Efficient, Hard-working, Well-organized	Easy-Going, Negligent, Lazy, Disorganized
Agreeableness	Friendly, Trusting, Lenient	Analytical, Ruthless, Critical
Neuroticism	Nervous, Emotional, Worried	Confident, Unemotional, Calm
Openness	Curious, Creative, Imaginative	Cautious, Conventional, Down-to-earth
Extraversion	Outgoing, Talkative, Active	Reserved, Loner, Quiet

What are your industry's standard direct and indirect channels?

Is the sales process documented and can it easily be communicated to sales people?

Is there an existing demand that partners can fulfill based on their skills and availability to customers?

What do you want to communicate with your channel?

Describe a closed standard/compatible network for your idea.

Describe a closed standard/incompatible network for your idea.

Describe an open standard/compatible network for your idea.

Describe an open standard/incompatible network for your idea.

Is your core process standardizable or original work?

What methodology would help you improve quality?

What metrics will you use to monitor performance?

What resources are critical for your plan?

Factor of Production	Description	Need
Capital	Tools and building	-
Land	Natural resources	-
Labor	Human efforts	-
Intellectual Property	Creations of the mind	-
Time	Duration of the process	-

Describe your output.

Describe your fixed costs and your variable costs.

Do you have an opportunity for economies of scale?

What is more important to you, rules or relationships?

Do you prefer to work in a group or as individual?

Do you display your emotions?

How separate do you keep your private and working life?

Do you have to prove yourself to receive status or is it given to you?

Do you do things one at a time or several things at once?

Do you control your environment or are does your environment control you?

Who are the essentials you need in your hierarchy?

How will you apply the rules of governance?

What is your vision for customer service?

Review your analysis in the other types. Do you need to make any changes to your vision or to your other types?

What combinations of types and grades of innovation would strengthen your idea?

Part 4: People

What expertise is required for your idea?

Give one or more examples of extrinsic motivation for your idea.

Give one or more examples of intrinsic motivation for your idea.

What is the role for a creative in your idea?

What is the role for a systematic in your idea?

What is the role for a bureaucrat in your idea?

Give me an example of a time you were in a mismatched role.

Do you have the right team for your idea?

Part 5: Organizational Structures

What structure is best for your idea?

Part 6: Diffusion Process

Who are your innovators?

Who are your early adopters?

Who are your industry non-adopters?

Describe your target social system.

What are the social norms of your targeted social system?

How is the social system structured?

How does the social system confer status?

How does the social system gossip?

ABOUT THE AUTHOR

In May 2011, I founded a healthcare data analytics company that I thought was guaranteed to succeed. For reasons unknown at the time, it was guaranteed to fail.

The company used software to analyze healthcare companies' data and found services they had provided to patients but, because of human error, never charged to insurance companies. My company was paid a percentage of any amounts the customers recovered, so they had no financial risk. I did so much right but, unknowingly, I made errors that kill innovation.

Since closing down the analytics company I began searching for answers, but no one could explain why it failed. I had to find the answers myself and the result is *Without Luck*, a step-by-step guide to approach all aspects of innovation. As I have discussed these ideas with other innovators and entrepreneurs, I realized how powerful the framework is and set out to spread them around the globe.

The framework is the foundation of d13 innovation consulting, a consulting firm I founded to support people who bring the best innovations into the world. I also volunteer as a mentor at USC Viterbi School of Engineering and as Entrepreneur-in-Residence for the CONNECT program, which aims to foster entrepreneurship in Southern California.

Before I founded the healthcare analytics company I led other successful innovation initiatives. I was the first hire with a telecom that grew revenue from $20 million to $150 million in four years. I have sold two companies I founded and had another project listed on The TIME 100 Most Influential Things in the World 2011.

My career has also allowed me to help nonprofits in various roles, where I contribute my time and talents to promote the common good and fulfill their missions.

NOTES

1

The Mind Behind Tesla, SpaceX, SolarCity ..., transcript of video interview of Elon Musk, TED, recorded February 2013, accessed August 15, 2017, https://www.ted.com/talks/elon_musk_the_mind_behind_tesla_spacex_solarcity.

2

Terence Irwin and Gail Fine, *Aristotle: Introductory Readings*, (Indianapolis: Hackett, 1996).

3

Kevin Rose, *Foundation 20 // Elon Musk*, YouTube video, September 7, 2012, https://www.youtube.com/watch?v=L-s_3b5fRd8.

4

Peter A. Thiel and Blake Masters, *Zero to One: Notes on Startups, or How to Build the Future*, (London:Virgin Books, 2015).

5

Sean M. Carroll, *From Eternity to Here: The Quest for the Ultimate Theory of Time*, (New York: Dutton, 2016).

6

Carroll, *From Eternity*.

7

David G. McCullough, *The Wright Brothers*, (New York: Simon & Schuster, 2016).

8

Congressional Budget Office, *Spending and Funding for Highways, Economic and Budget Issue Brief*, January 2011, accessed August 15, 2017, https://www.cbo.gov/sites/default/files/112th-congress-2011-2012/reports/01-19-highwayspending_brief.pdf.

9

FireflySixtySeven, *MaslowsHierarchyOfNeeds.svg*, digital image, Wikimedia Commons, November 2, 2014, accessed September 14, 2017, https://commons.wikimedia.org/wiki/File:MaslowsHierarchyOfNeeds.svg.
10

David Graeber, *The Utopia of Rules: On Technology, Stupidity, and the Secret Joys of Bureaucracy,* (Brooklyn: Melville House, 2016).
11

Clayton Christensen, *Disruptive Innovation*, October 23, 2012, accessed September 14, 2017, http://www.claytonchristensen.com/key-concepts/#sthash.Uqaulm5l.dpuf.
12

Centers for Disease Control and Prevention, *Use and Characteristics of Electronic Health Record Systems Among Office-based Physician Practices: United States, 2001–2013,* January 17, 2014, accessed September 14, 2017, http://www.cdc.gov/nchs/data/databriefs/db143.htm.
13

CME Group, *CME Group Overview*, 2013, accessed September 14, 2017, http://www.cmegroup.com/company/files/cme-group-overview.pdf.
14

CME Group, *Twenty Years of CME Globex*, 2012, accessed September 14, 2017, http://www.cmegroup.com/education/files/globex-retrospective-2012-06-12.pdf.
15

Lee Rainie and Jacob Poushter, Pew Research Center, *Emerging Nations Catching Up to U.S. on Technology Adoption, Especially Mobile and Social Media Use*, February 13, 2014, accessed September 14, 2017, http://www.pewresearch.org/fact-tank/2014/02/13/emerging-nations-catching-up-to-u-s-on-technology-adoption-especially-mobile-and-social-media-use/.
16

Julian F.V. Vincent et al., *Biomimetics: Its Practice and Theory*, Journal of the Royal Society Interface, April 18, 2006, retrieved April 7, 2015, https://www.researchgate.net/publication/6937083_Biomimetics_Its_Practice_and_Theory.
17

Clayton Christensen, *Disruptive Innovation*, October 23, 2012, accessed September 14, 2017, http://www.claytonchristensen.com/key-concepts/#sthash.Uqaulm5l.dpuf.
18

Peter A. Thiel and Blake Masters, *Zero to One: Notes on Startups, or How to Build the Future*, (London:Virgin Books, 2015).
19

Thomas Thurston, *Christensen: A Big Guy on the Shoulders of Giants*, Thomas Thurston (blog), November 30, 2015, accessed April 16, 2016, http://growthsci.com/blog/christensen-big-guy-shoulders-giants.
20

Megapixie, *Disruptive Technology Graph*, digital image, Wikipedia, October 18, 2005, accessed September 14, 2017, https://commons.wikimedia.org/wiki/File:Disruptivetechnology.png.
21

Clayton M. Christensen and Michael E. Raynor, *The Innovator's Solution: Creating and Sustaining Successful Growth*, (Boston: Harvard Business School, 2003).
22

Peter A. Thiel and Blake Masters, *Zero to One: Notes on Startups, or How to Build the Future*, (London:Virgin Books, 2015).
23

Bruce Gibney, *What Happened to the Future?*, Founders Fund, accessed September 14, 2017, http://foundersfund.com/the-future.`
24

Kim-Mai Cutler, *Why The Most Famously Libertarian VC Firm is Diving Deep Into Education And Health*, TechCrunch, June 22, 2015, accessed April 17, 2016, http://techcrunch.com/2015/06/22/singerman-health-education-founders-fund.

25

Tesla, *Tesla Energy*, press information, no publication date available, accessed March 14, 2016, https://www.teslamotors.com/presskit/teslaenergy.

26

Sun Tzu, *The Art of War: A New Translation,* (Boston: Shambhala, 2001).

27

Union of Concerned Scientists, *How Nuclear Power Works*, January 29, 2014, accessed September 14, 2017, http://www.ucsusa.org/our-work/nuclear-power/nuclear-power-101.

28

Standard and Poor's, *S&P Global Ratings Definitions*, June 26, 2017, accessed September 14, 2017, https://www.standardandpoors.com/en_US/web/guest/article/-/view/sourceId/504352.

29

Ascot Top Hats, *The First Silk Top Hat*, news release, June 16, 2009, accessed September 14, 2017, http://www.ascot-tophats.co.uk/News%20Release%20%20-%20The%20First%20Silk%20Top%20Hat.pdf.

30

Thornton, Richard H. "The First Silk Hat in London". *Notes and Queries* (s9-III), January 7, 1899, accessed September 14, 2017, https://play.google.com/books/reader?printsec=frontcover&output=reader&id=OSYwAQAAMAAJ.

31

Alexis C. Madrigal, *The Fall of Facebook*, The Atlantic, November 17, 2014, accessed September 14, 2017, https://www.theatlantic.com/magazine/archive/2014/12/the-fall-of-facebook/382247/.

32

Jan Brandt, *How Much Did It Cost AOL to Distribute All Those CDs Back in the 1990s? Whose Idea Was It?* Quora (blog), December 27,

2010, accessed September 14, 2017, https://www.quora.com/How-much-did-it-cost-AOL-to-distribute-all-those-CDs-back-in-the-1990s-Whose-idea-was-it.

33

Steve Case, *How Much Did It Cost AOL to Distribute All Those CDs Back in the 1990s? Whose Idea Was It?* Quora (blog), January 2, 2011, accessed September 14, 2017, https://www.quora.com/How-much-did-it-cost-AOL-to-distribute-all-those-CDs-back-in-the-1990s-Whose-idea-was-it.

34

Kathleen Roney, *If Interoperability is the Future of Healthcare, What's the Delay?* Becker's Health IT & CIO Review, December 20, 2012, accessed September 14, 2017, http://www.beckershospitalreview.com/healthcare-information-technology/if-interoperability-is-the-future-of-healthcare-whats-the-delay.html.

35

Elena Ferrante and Ann Goldstein, *The Story of the Lost Child,* (Waterville, ME: Thorndike Press, 2016).

36

Paul Sawers, *Dave McClure's 10 Tips for the Perfect Investment Pitch,* The Next Web. October 29, 2011, accessed September 14, 2017, https://thenextweb.com/entrepreneur/2011/10/29/dave-mcclures-10-tips-for-the-perfect-investment-pitch.

37

Liz Jacobs, *GPS, Lithium Batteries, the Internet, Cellular Technology, Airbags: A Q&A About How Governments Often Fuel Innovation,* TED Blog, October 30, 2014, accessed September 14, 2017, http://blog.ted.com/qa-mariana-mazzucato-governments-often-fuel-innovation.

38

Tom Simonite, *The Decline of Wikipedia,* MIT Technology Review. October 22, 2013, accessed September 14, 2017. https://www.technologyreview.com/s/520446/the-decline-of-wikipedia/.

39

Oded Nov, *What Motivates Wikipedians?* Communications of the ACM, November 2007, 60–64, https://cacm.acm.org/magazines/2007/11/5534-what-motivates-wikipedians/abstract.

40

Bloomberg, *Mark Cuban: Only Morons Start a Business on a Loan*, YouTube video, June 14, 2013, accessed September 14, 2017, https://www.youtube.com/watch?v=KYneLGRTgy8.

41

Jean-Noël Kapferer, *The New Strategic Brand Management Creating and Sustaining Brand Equity Long Term*, (London: Kogan, 2012).

42

O.P. John, L.P. Naumann, and C.J. Soto, *Paradigm Shift to the Integrative Big-Five Trait Taxonomy: History, Measurement, and Conceptual Issues*, in O. P. John, R. W. Robins, and L. A. Pervin, eds., *Handbook of Personality: Theory and Research*, (New York: Guilford Press, 2008).

43

Sanjay Srivastava, *Measuring the Big Five Personality Domains*, retrieved September 21, 2017, http://psdlab.uoregon.edu/bigfive.html.

44

Paul T. Costa Jr. and Robert R. McCrae, *Revised NEO Personality Inventory (NEO-PI-R) and NEO Five-Factor Inventory (NEO-FFI)*, (Odessa, FL: Psychological Assessment Resources, 1992).

45

Intuit, *Intuit Hits 50,000-member Milestone With QuickBooks ProAdvisor Program*, news release, June 19, 2008, accessed September 14, 2017, http://www.intuit.com/company/press-room/press-releases/2008/0619qb.

46

Ruth Laugesen, *From Xero a Hero*, Noted, October 17, 2013, accessed September 14, 2017, http://www.noted.co.nz/money/business/from-xero-a-hero/.

47

Wade Roush, *Kiwi Startup Xero Pries Accountants Away from Intuit's QuickBooks*, Xconomy, June 30, 2014, accessed September 14, 2017, http://www.xconomy.com/san-francisco/2014/06/30/kiwi-startup-xero-pries-accountants-away-from-intuits-quickbooks/.

48

Axel Schultze, *Channel Excellence: Architect, Manage and Accelerate Indirect Businesses,* (Morrisville, NC: Lulu.com, 2007).

49

Schultze, *Channel Excellence.*

50

Carl Shapiro and Hal R. Varian, *Information Rules: A Strategic Guide to the Network Economy,* (Boston: Harvard Business School Press, 2010).

51

Lily Prasuethsut, *Steam Rises to the Console Challenge with 65m Users, Surpassing Xbox Live,* TechRadar, October 23, 2013, accessed September 14, 2017, http://www.techradar.com/news/gaming/steam-rises-to-the-console-challenge-with-65m-users-surpasses-xbox-live-1195004.

52

James P. Womack and Daniel T. Jones, *Lean Thinking,* (New York: Free Press, 2003).

53

Hasso Plattner, Christoph Meinel and Larry J. Leifer, eds., *Design Thinking: Understand, Improve, Apply,* (Berlin, Heidelberg: Springer-Verlag, 2011).

54

Kent Beck at al., *Principles behind the Agile Manifesto,* Agile Alliance, 2001, http://agilemanifesto.org/principles.html

55

Mike Loukides, *What is DevOps?,* (O'Reilly Media, 2012).

56

Fons Trompenaars and Charles Hampden-Turner, *Riding the Waves of Culture,* (London: Nicholas Brealey Publishing, 1997).

57

Tyler Cowen, *A Conversation with Peter Thiel*, transcript and audio recording, Mecatus Center, April 6, 2015, accessed March 13, 2016, https://medium.com/conversations-with-tyler/peter-thiel-on-the-future-of-innovation-77628a43c0dd.

58

Britt Benston, *Peter Thiel on Startups, Buzzwords, and Complex Coordination*, blog, UCLA Anderson School of Management, January 26, 2015, accessed March 13, 2016, http://blogs.anderson.ucla.edu/anderson/2015/01/peter-thiel-on-startups-buzzwords-and-complex-coordination.html.

59

Peter A. Thiel and Blake Masters, *Zero to One: Notes on Startups, or How to Build the Future,* (London:Virgin Books, 2015).

60

Bill Chappell, *New Tesla Breaks Consumer Reports' Ratings Scale, Bolsters Company's Stock*, NPR, August 27, 2015, accessed March 13, 2017, http://www.npr.org/sections/thetwo-way/2015/08/27/435325951/new-tesla-breaks-consumer-reports-ratings-scale-bolsters-companys-stock.

61

Alexis Madrigal, *What Data Tesla Collects on Your Driving*, The Atlantic, November 5, 2010, https://www.theatlantic.com/technology/archive/2010/11/what-data-tesla-collects-on-your-driving/66173/

62

Tesla, *Factory Upgrade*, blog, November 17, 2014, accessed March 13, 2016, https://www.teslamotors.com/blog/factory-upgrade.

63

Job Hub: Tesla Motors Jobs and Culture, Management Consulted, August 23, 2015, accessed March 15, 2016, https://managementconsulted.com/consulting-jobs/job-hub-tesla-motors-jobs-and-culture.

64

Kim-Mai Cutler, *Q&A: Why The Most Famously Libertarian VC Firm is Diving Deep Into Education And Health*, TechCrunch, June 22, 2015, accessed March 13, 2016, http://techcrunch.com/2015/06/22/singerman-health-education-founders-fund.

65

Jim Collins, *Good to Great*. (New York: Harper Business, 2001).

66

Vator News, *Elon Musk: Work Twice as Hard as Others*, YouTube video, August 9, 2013, accessed September 15, 2017, https://www.youtube.com/watch?v=GtaxU6DZvLs.

67

Eric Schmidt, *How Google Works,* (New York: Grand Central Publishing, 2014).

68

Karen Martin, *The Outstanding Organization: Generate Business Results by Eliminating Chaos and Building the Foundation for Everyday Excellence,* (New York: McGraw-Hill, 2012).

69

Max Weber, *Wirtschaft und Gesellschaft*, (Tübingen, Mohr, 1922).

70

Marc Andreessen, *The Pmarca Blog Archives,* (Montreal: Pressbooks, 2015), http://pmarchive.com/guide_to_big_companies_part2.html, accessed September 15, 2017.

71

Sam Altman, *Startup Playbook*, no publication date available, accessed September 15, 2017, http://playbook.samaltman.com.

72

David Graeber, *The Utopia of Rules: On Technology, Stupidity, and the Secret Joys of Bureaucracy,* (Brooklyn, NY: Melville House, 2016).

73

Richard L. Brandt, "Birth of a Salesman," *The Wall Street Journal*, October 15, 2011, accessed September 15, 2017, http://online.wsj.com/article/SB10001424052970203914304576627102996831200.html.
74

Marc Andreessen, *The Pmarca Blog Archives,* (Montreal: Pressbooks, 2015) http://pmarchive.com/guide_to_big_companies_part1.html, accessed September 15, 2017.
75

A.D. Chandler Jr., Strategy and Structure: Chapters in the History of the American Industrial Enterprise, (Cambridge, MA: MIT Press), 1962.
76

Larry Page and Sergey Brin, *2004 Founders' IPO Letter*, Alphabet Investor Relations. Alphabet, Inc., August 18, 2004, accessed March 13, 2016, https://abc.xyz/investor/founders-letters/2004/ipo-letter.html.
77

Google for Work Security and Compliance Whitepaper, How Google Protects Your Data, Google, no publication date available, accessed March 12, 2016, https://static.googleusercontent.com/media/apps.google.com/en/US/files/google-apps-security-and-compliance-whitepaper.pdf.
78

G Suite, *Inside a Google Data Center*, YouTube video, December 16, 2014, accessed March 13, 2016, https://youtu.be/XZmGGAbHqa0.
79

Mike Loukides, *What is DevOps?* (O'Reilly Media, 2012).
80

Erich Floris, Amrit Chintan, and Daneva Maya, *A Mapping Study on Cooperation between Information System Development and Operations*, December 10, 2014, accessed March 14, 2016, https://ris.utwente.nl/ws/files/5293220/A_Mapping_Study_on_DevOps-Erich-Amrit-Daneva-PROFES2014.pdf.
81

Ashish Kumar, *Development at the Speed and Scale of Google*, Google, no publication date available, accessed March 14, 2016, https://qconsf.com/sf2010/dl/qcon-sanfran-2010/slides/AshishKumar_DevelopingProductsattheSpeedandScaleofGoogle.pdf.
82

Larry Page and Sergey Brin, *2004 Founders' IPO Letter*, Alphabet Investor Relations. Alphabet, Inc., August 18, 2004, accessed March 13, 2016, https://abc.xyz/investor/founders-letters/2004/ipo-letter.html.
83

Google Gets the Message, Launches Gmail, Google news release, April 1, 2004, accessed March 15, 2016, http://googlepress.blogspot.com/2004/04/google-gets-message-launches-gmail.html.
84

Harry McCracken, *How Gmail Happened: The Inside Story of Its Launch 10 Years Ago*, Time, April 1, 2014, accessed March 14, 2016, http://time.com/43263/gmail-10th-anniversary.
85

Form 10-K, United States Security and Exchange Commission, Alphabet, Inc., February 1, 2016, accessed March 12, 2016, https://abc.xyz/investor/pdf/20151231_alphabet_10K.pdf.
86

Google, *What Are the Global Faculty Research Awards?*, Research at Google, no publication date available, accessed March 15, 2016, https://research.google.com/research-outreach.html#/research-outreach/faq/faculty-research-awards.
87

Google, *What Are Focused Research Awards?*, Research at Google, no publication date available, accessed March 15, 2016, https://research.google.com/research-outreach.html#/research-outreach/faq/focused-research-awards.
88

Google, *What Are Google Earth Engine Research Awards?*, Research at Google, no publication date available, accessed March 15,

2016, https://research.google.com/research-outreach.html#/research-outreach/faculty-engagement/earth-engine-research-awards.

[89] Ross Koningstein, *And the Winner of the $1 Million Little Box Challenge Is...CE+T Power*, Google Research Blog, February 29, 2016, accessed March 14, 2016, http://googleresearch.blogspot.com/2016/02/and-winner-of-1-million-little-box.html.

[90] Google, *Detailed Inverter Specifications, Testing Procedure, and Technical Approach and Testing Application Requirements for the Little Box Challenge*, July 22, 2014, accessed March 14, 2016, https://www.littleboxchallenge.com/pdf/LBC-InverterRequirements-20150717.pdf.

[91] World Intellectual Property Organization, *Technology Licensing*, no publication date available, accessed March 15, 2016, http://www.wipo.int/sme/en/ip_business/licensing/technology_license.htm.

[92] Lockheed Martin, *Missions Impossible: The Skunk Works Story*, no publication date available, accessed March 12, 2016, http://www.lockheedmartin.com/us/100years/stories/skunk-works.html.

[93] Lockheed Martin, *Missions Impossible*, http://www.lockheedmartin.com/us/100years/stories/skunk-works.html.

[94] Form 10-K, United States Security and Exchange Commission, Alphabet, Inc., February 1, 2016, accessed March 12, 2016, https://abc.xyz/investor/pdf/20151231_alphabet_10K.pdf.

[95] Astro Teller, *The Secret to Moonshots? Killing Our Projects*, Backchannel, February 16, 2016, accessed March 13, 2016,

https://backchannel.com/the-secret-to-moonshots-killing-our-projects-49b18dc7f2d6#.6juxhk8gy.

96 Bill Maris, GV 2015 Year in Review, GV Library, December 6, 2015, accessed March 13, 2016, https://library.gv.com/gv-2015-year-in-review-5a6b61e37b5b#.304zrhrzb.

97 Claire Cain Miller, "Google Looks for the Next Google," *The New York Times*, July 19, 2011, accessed March 13, 2016, http://www.nytimes.com/2011/07/20/technology/google-spending-millions-to-find-the-next-google.html.

98 Sarah McBride, "Exclusive: Google Ventures Beefs up Fund Size to $300 Million a Year," *Reuters*, November 8, 2012, accessed March 13, 2016, http://www.reuters.com/article/us-venture-google-cash-idUSBRE8A70MD20121108.

99 John McDuling, *What It's like to Run Google's $2 Billion Venture Capital Fund*, Quartz. May 7, 2015, accessed March 15, 2016, http://qz.com/399232/what-its-like-to-run-googles-2-billion-venture-capital-fund.

100 Google, *Google To Acquire YouTube for $1.65 Billion in Stock*, news release, October 9, 2006, accessed March 13, 2016, http://googlepress.blogspot.com/2006/10/google-to-acquire-youtube-for-165_09.html.

101 Mike Swift, "Susan Wojcicki: The Most Important Googler You've Never Heard of," *The Mercury News*, February 3, 2011, accessed March 13, 2016, http://www.mercurynews.com/ci_17286427.

102 Form 10-K, United States Security and Exchange Commission, Alphabet, Inc., February 1, 2016, accessed March 12, 2016, https://abc.xyz/investor/pdf/20151231_alphabet_10K.pdf.

[103] Aristotle, *Politics,* (Chicago: University of Chicago Press, 2013).

[104] Robert D. Cialdini, "Crafting Normative Messages to Protect the Environment," *Current Directions in Psychological Science,* August 1, 2003, 105–109, http://journals.sagepub.com/doi/abs/10.1111/1467-8721.01242.

[105] Dacher Keltner, *The Power Paradox: How We Gain and Lose Influence,* (London: Penguin Books, 2017).

[106] Keltner, *The Power Paradox.*

[107] FireflySixtySeven, *MaslowsHierarchyOfNeeds.svg,* digital image, Wikimedia Commons, November 2, 2014, accessed September 14, 2017, https://commons.wikimedia.org/wiki/File:MaslowsHierarchyOfNeeds.svg.